A Study Guide to

E. Annie Proulx's

THE SHIPPING NEWS

Sophie Benkemoun, B.A., Dip.A.
Richard McRoberts, B.A., M.Ed., M.A.C.E.

WIZ★RD
BOOKS

First published in 1997 by
Wizard Books Pty Ltd
ACN 054 644 361
P.O. Box 304 Ballarat 3353 Australia
Email: wizard@netconnect.com.au
Website:www.wizardbooks.ballarat.net.au

ISBN 1 875739 57 2

Printed by Sands Print Group, Perth
Cover design by Cressaid Media, Ballarat

The Shipping News is published by Fourth Estate, London
© E. Annie Proulx 1993

BIOGRAPHICAL NOTES ON E. ANNIE PROULX

Born in Norwich, Connecticut, in 1935, E(dna) Annie Proulx (pronounced 'Pru'), was the oldest of five girls. Her mother came from a long line of farmers, mill workers and artists and her father was in the textile trade. Like many, Proulx's father detached himself from his French-Canadian background and 'reinvented himself as a New England Yankee'. As a result of his trade, the family moved frequently from place to place, and Proulx attended various schools.

Proulx lives in Vermont, though she has continued the itinerant lifestyle begun in her childhood. She enjoys travelling around North America, her favourite stops being Newfoundland and Wyoming. In fact, she claims that the best thing about writing is 'jumping in [her] pickup truck and taking off – stop[ping] along by a graveyard, writ[ing] some, and then sleep[ing] in the truck'.

Proulx began her writing career in freelance journalism. She graduated from the Sir George Williams University (now known as the Concordia University) in 1975, with an M.A. Degree and a doctorate in history. Faced with a lack of jobs in this field, Proulx launched into journalism, writing articles for numerous magazines, on subjects as diverse as apples, canoeing, mice, libraries, African beadwork, cider and lettuces. In addition to articles, Proulx wrote reviews and co-wrote a number of 'how-to-books' on subjects including cooking, gardening and self-sufficiency. This writing spanned over a decade, during which time Proulx was also raising three sons as a single parent. When she had extra time, she would write short stories, averaging two a year, and most of these were published in 1988 as a collection entitled *Heart Songs and Other Stories*.

Proulx came to writing fiction relatively late in her life, and she says that she is 'racing against the clock to get everything down', for her head is 'jammed with stories [that] are pushing to get out'. Since the 1980s, Proulx has gained much acclaim for her fiction writing. In 1992, with her first novel *Postcards*, Proulx was the first woman to win the PEN/Faulkner Award for Fiction, while *The Shipping News*, published in 1993, won the American National Book Award and a Pulitzer Prize for fiction, as well as the Irish Times International Fiction Award 'in recognition of her work as a novelist'.

Proulx's fascination with the outcome of people's lives when the 'rugs are yanked out from under them' coupled with poetic prose rich in dialectical and geographical detail, is at the core of her writing. Odd facts and local curiosities are woven with deft fingers amongst 'meticulously-researched histories' of the places and people she depicts in her stories.

Apart from writing full time, Proulx enjoys spending time outdoors, and engages in many activities including canoeing, walking, cross-country skiing, hunting grouse, and searching for mushrooms and wildflowers. She lives by herself, now that her sons are grown and has no desire for the 'jolly family circle'. Proulx has found her niche and is happy to remain outside of the mainstream, from where she can observe life and accomodate her own interests and routine. For Proulx, 'Home is where the words are – and wherever she is, there will be words, stories to untangle.'

THE TEXT IN PERSPECTIVE...
NOTES ON GENRE, STRUCTURE & STYLE

At one level, and most obviously, *The Shipping News* is a psychological drama. It tracks the fortunes of its central character, Quoyle, from his low point in New York State, the victim of a dysfunctional family, occasional unemployment, chronically low self-esteem, and a brutally unhappy marriage, through to his final development into a happily married man in Newfoundland. Although there are a great many elements mixed into this novel, the story is at heart the study of the growth and emerging fulfilment of an individual. The individual stories of other characters are woven cunningly by Proulx around the main story, elaborating on certain aspects of Quoyle's life, and in some cases, setting up useful contrasts. It is to Quoyle however, that we must return in summing up the book.

Yet *The Shipping News* is not entirely, or not only, a 'straight' psychodrama. More subversive but also more entertaining elements are involved. The novel is a comedy, of character, of manners and of situation. Many readers may find this aspect of the text difficult to appreciate, at least in the early chapters, which seem anything but funny. Yet the clues to the comic nature of Proulx's text are many. Consider the names alone: Agnis Hamm, Petal Bear, Tertius Card, Beety Buggit, Diddy Shovel, B. Beaufield Nutbeem, Mavis Bangs, Al Catalog, amongst others. Consider the sheer farce of many episodes (black humour though they may be): the suicide note of Quoyle's parents, left on his answering machine (but cut off by the beep); the selling of Bunny and Sunshine to an inept paedophile; the night and day during which Quoyle and his family are trapped in a motel room by a doorknob; the beheading of the obnoxious Melville by his adulterous wife, whose head is then washed up in a suitcase for Quoyle to find; the destruction of Nutbeem's boat by the wellwishers at his sendoff party; the storm which blows the Quoyle homestead back into the sea, whence it originally came; the death and resurrection of Jack Buggit. Consider the way Quoyle tends to think in headlines: MAN WITH HANGOVER LISTENS TO BOAT-BUILDER PROJECT VARIABLES, REPORTER LICKS EDITOR'S BOOT, etc. At times the comedy is overt, as in the Christmas pageant. At times it is buried beneath what looks like horror, as in the death of Petal. But it is there constantly. Is Proulx arguing something? The human condition as a comedy? Or is it just part of the 'upbeat' quality of her slant on life? Perhaps she is suggesting that dark moments can be lived through more easily if we perceive them with a sense of humour, if we appreciate the irony of life's events. There are dark substrata, of course – sexual abuse, death, poverty and so on. Acknowledging the darkness of her comedy, Proulx described her tone in the novel as 'light blue'. But the reader finishes *The Shipping News* feeling that despite hardship, there *is* hope, and that one ought to look for the positive in life, not just the negative. It is very much the moral that Quoyle himself has had to learn.

Finally, and working in seamlessly with the other two textual conventions already mentioned, we might consider *The Shipping News* as a slightly 'magical' narrative, a fable with a happy ending. As one reviewer perceptively remarked:

The Shipping News is the story of...a ne'er-do-well who finally does do well when he leaves behind his dreary, incommodious life in Mockingburg, New York, and returns to his ancestral country, the coast of Newfoundland....In a town called Killick-Claw, Quoyle finds competence and the respect of his neighbors and a good wife. The book's final sentence is this: 'And it may be that love sometimes occurs without pain or misery.' If this were the first sentence of the novel, the reader would know from the start what at first he only suspects: that *The Shipping News* is a fairy tale, a book that doesn't just happen to turn out happily but that plainly intends to turn out happily all the way, a book that is unstinting, almost, at times, forced, in its good cheer.

(Verlyn Klinkenborg, 'The Princess of Tides', *New Republic*, 30 May 1994)

Perhaps 'fairy tale' is too strong, but there is certainly something about the story which goes beyond realism and comedy. There is a gentle sense of destiny being worked out in a larger scheme of things. Jack's 'second sight' and miraculous salvation of Quoyle, as well as his own 'resurrection', are the most obvious examples, but the whole narrative sketches in a subtle 'Cinderella' sort of argument, in Quoyle, and perhaps in more muted form in Agnis and Wavey. The book ends on a note of tremendous hope. 'For if Jack Buggit could escape from the pickle jar, if a bird with a broken neck could fly away, what else might be possible?' Life as magical, after all, despite its tragedies? The suggestion that happy endings are possible? Maybe nothing more than this, but it adds another dimension to the text, and great charm.

Structurally, the book is quite conventional, its thirty-nine chapters marking out episodes in the central story of Quoyle. Interestingly, each has a distinguishing title, many taken from *The Ashley Book of Knots*. The chosen knot for a particular chapter is symbolic of the sort of subject matter treated in that chapter (e.g. 'Love knot', the chapter about Quoyle's encounter with Petal), although locations, fragments of dialogue, names or other signifying titles are also used. Naming the chapters in this way is a curiously old-fashioned and satisfying technique of identifying for the reader, at once teasing and revealing, what the author's subject matter is.

Stylistically, the book is quite remarkable. First of all, there is Proulx's unforgettable prose style, what one reviewer called 'the poetic extravagance of the narrator's voice'. Here is what another described as her brilliant use of language:

Its syllables urge and slice and spin the reader like a dervish wind. Salty, luscious, mind-grabbing, chewable words and phrases like dreary, Nutbeem, and the terrible Nightmare Isles energise the people and events. No avid reader can help but be drawn around and down into language's whirlpool.

(B.A. St. Andrews, Review in *World Literature Today*, Spring 1995)

Full of short, sharp sentences, often with the verbs suppressed, sometimes conversational in tone, sometimes sensuously poetic, always vigorous and gutsy, her style has been much commented on by critics. Some have even suggested that is is so strong it distracts the reader from the narrative. Be that as it may, she is a unique stylist and a great part of the charm of the book is the tremendous colour of the language.

Perhaps equally remarkable is her pervasive use of symbolism. The Anglo-American poet T. S. Eliot invented the term 'objective correlative' to describe the idea of an author representing inner states often too complex for description, in easy to understand external details. *The Shipping News* is full of this sort of technique. Most obviously perhaps, there is the landscape, which, while a literal thing of rock and water, also comes to evoke psychic states. The harshness of the Newfoundland coast, wave and storm-lashed, rocky and wet, after a while seems to us like a parallel to the nature of human existence – often turbulent, cruel, and bare of comfort. The seasons are partly used to evoke the mental state of Proulx's characters. The warm balmy days of late summer are, for example, linked to Quoyle first becoming physically close to Wavey. The ferocious winters by contrast are associated with the misfortune and hardship of other characters, such as the death of Jack's son. The need of the Newfoundland people to protect themselves indoors, to sustain one another in a warm bond of community against the sheer savagery of the elements, parallels the idea of people sharing in the bonds of friendship and mutual support against an often harsh fate.

Parallels of this kind abound in the novel. There is Quoyle's boat, like himself ill-designed, prone to disaster, and suffering what many see as an inevitable end. Although Quoyle himself survives and indeed flourishes, the boat has evoked for him and for us his sense of personal inadequacy. There is the old Quoyle house, lashed to the storm-ravished rock above the sea, again singularly evocative of the survival of the Quoyle family. There are, most noticeably, the knots.

> [The novel's] central metaphor and motif is the knot, the handmade contrivance that mediates between water and land, tying down all that would otherwise float away....[All the constant references to knots] would be mere arcana [clever but useless information] if it did not reinforce the book's larger theme: that commitment both binds us and holds us fast. For Quoyle, a fumble-fingered man, the triumph comes in learning to fashion sound knots.
>
> (Barbara Dafoe Whitehead, Critics Choices, *Commonweal*, 1 December 1995)

There are the knots which pepper the chapter titles, the knots left by Nolan, the knots tied by Bunny – all conjuring up in their way the concept of interconnections – intertwinings of lives, of emotions, hereditary and fate. There is finally the symbolism of *The Gammy Bird*, the newspaper for which Quoyle works. Its steady formula of accidents, gossip, scandal and shipping news, seems at first glance like a summary of life itself – the emphasis being on the dark side of existence. In it, as Nutbeem reveals (Chapter 27), the newspaper has almost become a type of therapy, not only for the people working on it, but presumably for the people who read it daily. Facing the horrors which fill its pages is a type of catharsis, a confronting of one's fears in order to overcome them. In short, the paper ultimately reflects a parallel with the psychic transformation taking place in Quoyle and others in the novel.

Dominated by its powerful portraits of individuals, its remarkably visualized evocation of place, its weaving of conventional structural elements with a uniquely poetic and colourful style, *The Shipping News* offers a rich mixture which has pleased critics around the world. Proulx is now considered one of America's most important contemporary writers, and this, her most famous work, is well deserving of serious study.

SYNOPSIS AND COMMENTARY
ON *THE SHIPPING NEWS*

Chapter 1   QUOYLE

Quoyle is a large, awkward man, who on account of a taunting brother and a relentlessly critical father, has a strong sense of his own failure. This failure stems from an unusual appearance. He is very big, unattractive and with a jutting chin which he covers self-consciously with his hand in the presence of others.

Quoyle is a hack journalist who arrived at the position quite by default through Partridge, a copy editor for a small town newspaper, the *Mockingburg Record*. Quoyle and Partridge met at the Mockingburg laundromat and began a friendship involving weekends spent with Partridge and his wife Mercalia. Although Quoyle continues to write poorly even after six months with the paper, he feels a sense of belonging and begins to feel, for the first time, that he is in control of his life.

After six months, Quoyle is 'laid off'. This begins a pattern of being fired, taking up part-time work, and being re-hired by the *Mockingburg Record*. The paper's managing editor Ed Punch has noticed that Quoyle inspires talkers, because his attentiveness 'juic[es] the life stories out of strangers'. This continuous pattern is accompanied by a dreary routine of writing his pieces, watching TV, dreaming of love, and bingeing.

When Partridge announces that he and Mercalia are leaving town, because Mercalia has accepted the New Orleans truck run, Quoyle doesn't want to let them go. Quoyle remains stuck in his insular world, oblivious to outside news – the environmental, political and social concerns of the world. He is waiting for his life to begin.

The Quoyle we meet at the opening of the book is a failure. An unhappy childhood with indifferent parents, a cruel brother, and his own sense of being 'different' on account of his size and his ugliness (specifically his large chin), Quoyle has grown up with a severe inferiority complex. With chronically low self-esteem, he has difficulty making anything of his life. His employment comes about seemingly by accident, and he is not very good at it; likewise his friendship with Partridge. At the outset, Quoyle is as low as he can be, a miserable loser. That this is going to change, and indeed be the principal psychological interest of the novel, is something that comes to us as the story progresses.

Chapter 2   LOVE KNOT

At a meeting, Quoyle sees Petal Bear, an attractive woman who is 'thin, moist, hot'. He is struck by her appearance and her provocative manner.

Petal and Quoyle marry. Quoyle expects 'happiness', but Petal soon betrays him with a string of affairs. She cannot stand his hesitancy or his hopeless devotion to her. When their first child Bunny is born, Petal is uninterested. Four days after the birth, she leaves for one of her love affairs. The following year a second child, Sunshine, is born, and it is Quoyle who takes responsibility for the two girls. He takes them everywhere with him, and does the housework in secret so that Petal cannot admonish him for accusing her of not doing it.

Quoyle pitifully accepts Petal's absence and cruelty, even when she rings up from Alabama for a cocktail recipe and hangs up in his ear, or when she arrives home and pretends not to recognise the children. He pines for Petal and refuses a divorce. Even when Petal brings a lover home, Quoyle wallows in silent misery instead of confronting her.

Just as he's a failure in his working life, so too is Quoyle a failure in love. His marriage to the sexually predatory Petal is a disaster. His pathetic adoration of her is met only by her undisguised contempt. He suffers abominably and can do nothing about it. Quoyle's first experience of love serves to convince him that the whole idea is fraught with danger. He is no hero, but he is a plainly a decent and good man, whom fate has treated badly. His very gentleness is a major reason Petal is able to mistreat him so. Increasingly, we come to sympathise with the unfortunate Quoyle, and hope that something good may come of his miserable existence.

Chapter 3   STRANGLE KNOT

Quoyle's parents become sick. His father is diagnosed with liver cancer and his mother is suffering from a brain tumour. They plan and carry out a deliberate suicide. Quoyle receives a message on his answering machine, saying that it is time for them to go and notifying Quoyle of the funeral arrangements, mentioning that Quoyle should contact Agnis Hamm, his aunt, and only traceable relative.

Quoyle contacts his brother Dicky, who states that he won't be coming to the funeral. Nor does Agnis Hamm come to the funeral; however, Quoyle receives a letter to inform of her arrival the following month.

The aunt's arrival coincides with another disaster – Petal has taken the children. A few days later, Ed Punch lays Quoyle off for good. Agnis Hamm listens intently as Quoyle sobs and talks and then she gives Quoyle a little insight into the family history in Newfoundland.

Quoyle is shocked when he receives a phone call from the police informing him of Petal's death in an accident and the whereabouts of his daughters. Petal had sold the children to a photographer the morning before. Fortunately, the children have not been sexually abused. When reunited, the girls rush at Quoyle, and he tells them he loves them.

In the midst of these troubled circumstances, Quoyle invites his aunt to stay with him and the children. She agrees to stay for a few days to help straighten things out. The aunt introduces Warren, her old dog.

Disaster is heaped upon disaster. His parents die, his brother rejects him anew, and he loses his job. His children have disappeared and then the wife he loved so much is

*killed in a shocking accident. Quoyle is broken-hearted, his life seemingly in total
ruin. Can he survive? Is there any possibility left for happiness?*

*The first ray of light is hearing that his children are safe and unharmed. He
adores them and it is the first piece of good news he has had. Although it is not clear at
the outset, the second piece of good news is the appearance of Aunt Agnis, who is to be
in Quoyle's life a major force for the attainment of happiness.*

Chapter 4   CAST AWAY

The aunt convinces Quoyle that there is nothing for him in Mockingburg anymore: he
is unemployed and his wife and parents are gone. Quoyle is eligible to claim $50,000
in insurance, so he agrees to head for the home of his ancestors, Newfoundland, to
make a fresh start.

Before leaving, Quoyle contacts his friend Partridge, who offers to try and set
up some work for Quoyle somewhere in the vicinity of the only nearby town, in prox-
imity to the family home, Killick-Claw. He gives Quoyle the name of Tertius Card,
editor of a weekly paper which is looking for someone to cover the shipping news.

After a long car trip north, Quoyle, the children, his aunt and Warren are on a
ferry headed for Newfoundland. The aunt is nostalgic, reminiscing about her childhood, with its hardship, hopelessness, and isolation, and wondering who has changed
more, 'place or self?'

*The journey back to Newfoundland is the product of apparently hopeless circum-
stances, in a sense a flight of despair. In another sense, as the aunt makes clear, it is a
'coming home'. Newfoundland is where the Quoyles came from, and as they make
their way back, we wonder if it will the beginning of a new phase for them – the chance
to start anew.*

Chapter 5   A ROLLING HITCH

Once in Newfoundland, they look for the old house. Eventually they find the turnoff to
Quoyle's Point. As the car bounces along the potted and rocky road Quoyle, wonders
whether anyone has ever gone over the edge. Cramped and uncomfortable, they spend
the night en route and continue in the morning, discovering that the road leads to a
carpark and a concrete building. From here, through a gap in the fog, the aunt sees that
the old house is still standing. The aunt is emotional with recollections. The old family
house, despite its disrepair, floods her with memories, and she vows that nothing will
drive her out a second time.

After breakfast on an outside fire and a walk around, Bunny asks Quoyle whether
Petal is going to live with them anymore. Quoyle is forced to remind her that Petal is
asleep in heaven, though he never says the word 'dead'. While Bunny is alone and
exploring the house's surroundings, she sees a strange white dog with matted fur and
gleaming eyes which scares her to shrieking. Although Quoyle searches for the dog, it
has vanished.

Their first sight of the old Quoyle house is anything but a romantic return. The place is derelict, and stands alone on a terrible windswept rock, miles from anywhere. At this point, Quoyle has no attachment to the place, but the aunt's enthusiasm leads him towards a tentative commitment. Ramshackle as it may be, it is in a sense 'home', a place which instils in Quoyle a sense of belonging, which comes to be one of the significant sub-textual ideas in the book.

Chapter 6   BETWEEN SHIPS

Quoyle does not think they can live in the family house, but the aunt believes they can. The aunt agrees that they will need to rent a house for a few months, during which time they will set about renovating, establishing the girls, and settling into their own work. Quoyle discovers that his aunt is an upholsterer.

At Ig's Store (on the main road), the aunt asks about the concrete building: a glove factory which had closed years before. As they leave the store, a shrieking wind gusts through, bringing with it a blizzard shooting from the east.

They make their way to a motel. The desk clerk informs them that there's only one room left; the storm has brought many in and it's darts playoff night. The motel room is ghastly, with broken facilities, and despite the aunt's optimism about a good meal and a decent night's sleep, these prove out of reach. A terrible night, punctuated by Bunny waking sobbing from a nightmare, precedes a day where they find themselves locked in the motel room on account of the doorknob having come off in Quoyle's hand. Banging on the door only arouses angry shouts from other guests and the phone is dead. The aunt writes a message on a pillow case and hangs it out the window. Finally the desk clerk comes to unlock the door.

As the tests of Quoyle's patience and optimism continue to pile up – the miserable old ruined house, the storm, the appalling motel where they are overcharged and given shockingly bad service – we laugh at the black humour of it all, but also perhaps note in passing that the family continues to endure. This capacity to endure will be equally important to their eventual success, and one of the human characteristics silently underlined and endorsed in the larger picture by the author.

Chapter 7   THE GAMMY BIRD

Quoyle is driving through the rain to Flour Sack Cove and the newspaper office when he notices a woman in a green raincoat holding the hand of a child. He waves, but she doesn't see.

At the newspaper office, Tert Card, editor of *The Gammy Bird*, invites Quoyle in, and introduces the team: Billy Pretty, a old man in his seventies, responsible for the Home News, and B. Beaufield Nutbeem, an Englishman, a deft hand at stealing foreign news stories from the short wave radio and rewriting them. Card points to a corner partitioned off with particleboard to indicate the boss, Mr Jack Buggit's, office.

Assigned his desk, Quoyle is told to sit tight and wait for Jack. Card advises Quoyle to acquaint himself with back copies of the paper, to learn the four main roads and turn up every morning. Spending the next week reading back issues of *The Gammy Bird*, Quoyle is astounded at the number of ads in the paper. As he turns the pages, Quoyle becomes familiar with the paper's formula: a car wreck on the front page, several sexual abuse stories in every issue, a restaurant review and the shipping news (a list of vessels in the port or leaving port). There is also a salacious gossip column, beating any he has ever read. Quoyle doesn't know how to write such stuff; it is nothing like the *Mockingburg Record*.

On the second Monday at the paper, Quoyle notices Jack Buggit in his office and goes in to meet him. Jack explains the background of the paper, how the Buggits settled in Flour Sack Cove, fished and sealed and did anything else to stay alive. He explains how when the Canadian Government took control of Newfoundland, the fishing began to decline, so he had gone to the Canada Manpower (employment) office asking what they had for him to do. After four jobs in various factories lined up by the organisation, interspersed with fishing, Jack got the idea to set up a newspaper. With money from Canada Manpower, he started the paper, and it works because he knows what people want to read.

Jack gives Quoyle the run down of what he is to cover: car wrecks and shipping news. Quoyle wonders how he is going to manage, queasy at the thought of blood and dying people and painfully aware of his inexperience with ships.

Finding his way to his new place of employment, Quoyle realises that this is no high-brow publication. The Gammy Bird *is a gossip rag, staffed by a crew of misfits and eccentrics, its pages filled with appallingly sensational material – wrecks, sexual abuse, and slander. Run by a fisherman of intermittent employment, it is about as low as a newpaper can go.*

This is in a sense yet another test. Will Quoyle baulk at its sheer squalour? No. He has nowhere else to go. And we should note as readers that while Proulx is satirising The Gammy Bird, *her humour is cheerful and indulgent. We may be appalled by the subject matter of the paper, but we cannot help noticing the humour with which Proulx treats it.*

We also note that in some symbolic way it mirrors the rather grisly subject matter of the story so far, perhaps in exaggerated form. While the argument should not be overdone, in some sense The Gammy Bird *represents a distillation of all the disasters in life. But is real life really like the pages of* The Gammy Bird? *Will Quoyle's story continue to be a series of disasters, as found in this rather grotesque publication, or will he find other aspects of life? We wait to find out.*

Chapter 8   A SLIPPERY HITCH

Back in the motel room, the children are squabbling. Quoyle is complaining that he doesn't think he can handle the job. The aunt hotly rebuffs Quoyle by saying of course he can handle the job; he has no choice, he has a family to bring up.

Quoyle hears his aunt talking about Dennis Buggit, a carpenter who has offered to do the work on the old house, and his wife, Beety, who is thinking of starting up day-care in her house. The aunt says that what they really need is a boat.

Quoyle asks Nutbeem about Dennis Buggit. Tert Card tells him that Dennis is Jack's youngest son, who was the apple of his father's eye, especially after they lost their eldest son, but not any more. Billy Pretty and Nutbeem advise Quoyle on getting a boat, and get lost in their own stories. Nutbeem ignores Pretty's interruptions and tells his story of touring from Texas to Los Angeles on a push bike, when the only thing that kept him going was the thought of a little sailboat he planned to get when he arrived.

Jack rings the office to speak with Quoyle, wanting to know what stories he has covered so far and reminding him not to forget the shipping news for the week. Quoyle is pleased that he has to go to the wharf, for at least there he won't have to witness accidents.

Quoyle has his predictable moment of fear, wondering how he can go on. Jack has asked him to cover car wrecks, which bring to mind his greatest trauma. It has pressed close on his life already. His nerve fails, and significantly it is his resilient aunt who pushes him back towards his duty. Although he dismisses her advice as 'ten cent philosophy' (homely wisdom), he later takes her advice on board, and we cannot help but agree that this is the best option. This is to be a story about simple people and simple virtues. Quoyle is learning already that, no matter how great the demands placed on him, he has a duty to survive and protect those he loves.

This chapter begins to introduce us also to some of the other eccentric characters now surrounding the Quoyle family. Once again we should be careful about judging them. Initially grotesque, they come after a time to seem like 'salt of the earth' individuals, real people (however fictional), whose unselfconscious wackiness is part of their zest for living, a zest which Quoyle will eventually find contagious.

Chapter 9   THE MOORING HITCH

At the harbour, Quoyle meets Diddy Shovel, the harbourmaster. Diddy offers him a note book with the word 'Arrivals' on its cover, and later, a book with 'Departures' on the front. It turns out that Diddy also has a computer. He explains that the two ways of recording information are to avoid any being lost when the power goes out during a storm. He offers Quoyle a cup of tea and talks.

Diddy learns that Quoyle's ancestors came from Quoyle's Point. Quoyle is uncomfortable talking about his background, so he changes the subject of conversation to a ship in the bay. The particular boat, the *Polar Grinder*, Diddy explains, caused the rift between Jack Buggit and his youngest son Dennis. Despite Jack's attempt to keep his son away from the sea, Dennis gained an appreticeship as carpenter on the vessel. Jack's fear of the sea had been validated when his eldest son Jesson was drowned at sea. One winter, many ships were caught and destroyed in a terrible storm, including the *Polar Grinder*, with Dennis on it. Everyone abandoned her. In the middle of his story the phone rings and the converstion is cut short.

Quoyle notices a small boat for sale. The owner says he can have it for a hundred dollars. The boat looks practically new. The man accepts Quoyle's offer of fifty dollars. Quoyle hires a trailer, ignoring the men who have gathered around to laugh. On his way back to *The Gammy Bird*, Quoyle notices the woman in the green raincoat and they wave at one another.

Back at the newspaper Jack asks Quoyle why he bought the boat. Quoyle is confused, because everyone has been at him to buy a boat, until he realises that he's bought a lemon: a boat with all the wrong curves, that is sure to sink.

We have already heard about the rift between Jack Buggit and his son Dennis. Now, from Diddy, we begin to hear the story. It amounts to this: Jack has already lost one son to the sea, and feared, in the incident of Polar Grinder, that he would lose his other son, Dennis. This is no romantic view of the sea, no fair weather sailor's fantasy of nature. The sea, in this novel, is a brutal and overwhelming force. It takes lives. It plays no favourites. While not overdoing the analogy, we begin to see as the book progresses that the sea, the elements, are like life itself. They are unpredictable and often cruel. One must be careful to survive, and find comfort in what one has.

The matter of Quoyle's ridiculous boat is the beginning of a considerable saga. Tricked by a sly local into buying an unseaworthy craft, the unfortunate Quoyle is exposed to ridicule once again, for the local men of the sea know the boat is a death trap. The boat may be taken as some sort of partial metaphor for Quoyle himself. Quoyle's own life has been a disaster. His very body is an 'unseaworthy craft', a grotesque and somewhat unworkable form. He has proved disaster-prone. What is to happen to Quoyle's boat, and its eventual replacement, is to work out in an almost metaphoric way the developing story of Quoyle himself. Quoyle may be at the outset a 'weak vessel', but by the end he will be a strong and seaworthy craft.

Chapter 10   THE VOYAGE OF NUTBEEM

Quoyle returns to the motel to find his aunt miserable. Her dog Warren has died. The aunt says she will part with Warren at sea.

His aunt explains that the Quoyle house can be ready in two weeks if someone helps Dennis with the repairs. She has organised to have an extra room in the motel. She explains that the house will take until autumn to complete, and that they'll need a dock to bring building materials across by boat – a lot faster than by road.

As Quoyle is telling his aunt about the boat he has bought, Nutbeem appears. He wants to finish the story about his boat. Over dinner, Nutbeem talks about his boating experiences and how he came to have an ugly, large boat based on the design of a Chinese junk. Nutbeem drones on about his journey across the Atlantic at the beginning of his world trip. The aunt leaves to be alone, and to take care of Warren.

Quoyle asks about the *Polar Grinder*. Nutbeem tells him that Jack is a 'weird chap [who] can read your mind'. Quoyle hears how the Search and Rescue crew had to abandon the search despite the fact that four men, including Dennis, were still lost. When they told Jack, he exclaimed that Dennis was alive, and he knew where to find him. Jack went out alone and brought Dennis back to shore. Jack said that if Dennis went out again, he'd drown himself. Nevertheless, as soon as his broken arms were healed, Dennis was back at sea. Nutbeem says that's the reason the two don't talk to one another.

Meanwhile, the aunt drives up the coast, looking for a good spot to farewell Warren. She thinks of her partner Irene Warren, for whom the dog was named. She thinks about how much she misses Irene as Warren glides out to sea in the sunset.

Quoyle had been challenged by The Gammy Bird, *adding to his already turbulent, traumatic life. The aunt is now challenged. The death of the dog, clearly very dear to her, is a test thrown up by fate, a test of her endurance and optimism. She not only mourns the dog, but we realise that its death recalls her own bereavement after the premature death of her lover Irene Warren. In the increasingly complex portrait of the aunt we see an example of Proulx's skill as a writer. Agnis is not the stereotyped little old lady we might have been to tempted to suspect – she has her own troubled past, her own buffetting by fate. As we watch her consign the dog to the sea, we feel a deepening sympathy for her predicament.*

Chapter 11   A BREASTPIN OF HUMAN HAIR

The aunt arrives at the family house on Quoyle's Point in her new pick-up truck. The road is fixed and the dock is in. There is an outhouse, the water is connected and the place is liveable. She is very excited to be there. She wanders through the rooms. She gets her brother's ashes from an upstairs room and dumps them in the toilet hole.

Next morning, Quoyle and the girls arrive. Proudly the aunt shows them the renovations. Dennis is on the roof hammering shingles. In the afternoon Bunny helps Quoyle with further renovations.

In the evening the aunt wants everyone to play cards, but the children don't understand the game and Quoyle would rather read.

Quoyle wakes in the early morning light in an empty room, pulls on his clothes and goes out. Something draws his attention to a texture caught in a cleft of rock. He frees it to discover that it is a brooch made of human hair. Repulsed, he throws it out to sea.

A storm is approaching and Quoyle is reluctant to get up onto the roof. He is awkward at first, but realises that it becomes easier as he goes along. Suddenly Bunny appears on the ladder, at roof level, with a hammer in her hand. Quoyle imagines Bunny plunging to the rock below. He fixes her to the spot with his voice, urging her to wait. As he grasps her, the hammer falls to the ground. With his arms about his daughter, Quoyle descends the ladder with trembling legs, reliving the image of her potential death.

We should note the aunt's joy at the restoration of her old family home. It is a reflection on the theme (already noted) about belonging and return. Lest we become too sentimental about family and roots, however, we are offered the bizarre detail of the Aunt taking her brother's (Quoyle's father's) ashes and consigning them to the toilet, then proceeding to urinate on them. The reason for this bizarre behaviour is utterly mysterious at this point. Chapter 36 will eventually provide us with the final ugly piece in the Quoyle jigsaw.

Everything appears to be proceeding normally and positively in the Quoyle household. Two matters however remind us that the appearance of calm and benign good fortune are not the whole of the story. The first thing is the set of knots left around the house, one of which gives the chapter its name. Is it some sort of curse? What knotted problems from past or present hang over the Quoyle dynasty? Once again we will need to wait till considerably later in the story to find out.

The other dark possibility is that of death again. Quoyle suddenly sees, when Bunny comes up the ladder to the steep roof, the possiblity of her being killed. The possible injury of his daughter renews his terrors of death. Yet we can take this another way, and in the spirit of the chapter, should. The girl could have died, but didn't. He, by quick thinking and resolve, saved her. Forthright action prevented tragedy. He has asserted himself at the most basic level – the instinctive need to protect a loved one. And the girl lives on, comically squabbling and wriggly with vitality. Death has been averted. Death does not always have its way.

Chapter 12   THE STERN WAVE

Quoyle gets his boat into the water, starts the motor, and sets off, gaining confidence as he begins to control her. At a sharp turn, water splashes into the boat. Water continues to fill the boat and there is nothing with which to empty it out. Quoyle returns to the dock and goes back to the house for a coffee can to empty the water from the boat.

Nutbeem knows why the boat fills with water – it is cut too low. He advises Quoyle on all the things he has to get for the boat. Dennis advises Quoyle that even if they fix the boat, he should only go out on calm days. He suggests that Quoyle go and see Alvin Yark about making him a good boat.

The boat, as we have already noted, a somewhat symbolic object, demonstrates again its unsuitability. Quoyle accepted it out of ignorance and now finds that his experience matches the dire predictions. Thus also, his life so far, a misshapen and unsuccessful thing has lived up to the worst possibilities. He needs a new boat. He needs a new life.

Chapter 13   THE DUTCH CRINGLE

Diddy Shovel rings, telling Quoyle to come down to the wharf to catch a glimpse of a boat, the likes of which he will never again see. It is 'Hitler's boat' and the owner says the press is welcome to have a look. Billy, excited, goes with him.

In the car, Quoyle passes the woman in the green raincoat, and her son. Their eyes meet. Quoyle asks Billy who she is and Billy replies that they should have stopped to give her a lift. He explains that the woman and child are returning from a special class at the school as the boy's 'not right'. Billy thinks that grief caused the child's condition as the woman's husband was lost at sea while she was pregnant. Quoyle gives them a lift, and Billy introduces them: Wavey and Herry Prowse. Quoyle drops them off at a house with painted wooden and metal sculptures out the front. Wavey explains that the sculptures are her dad's. Quoyle is taken by her.

At the wharf, they find the boat to which Diddy was referring, *Tough Baby*. A man, Bayonet Melville, emerges from the cabin. Hearing they are from the local paper, he agrees to show them around despite being in the middle of an argument with his wife. The boat is a traditional, flat bottomed Dutch barge which had belonged to Hitler, but had been a wreck when he had bought her. The interior is decorative and expensive looking. A dishevelled woman, Silver Melville, is there. The man starts to tell the story of Hurricane Bob, recounting how, at the height of a storm, *Tough Baby* slipped her moorings and smashed seventeen boats, before demolishing twelve beach houses (when the waves pushed her aground). The only damage sustained to the boat was a cracked lee board. Quoyle asks what brings them to Killick-Claw. The man replies that they have only come to this 'godforsaken' place as his wife insists on having a particular upholsterer work on the furniture: Agnis Hamm.

The appearance of Wavey in Quoyle's life is a vital one. He has already noticed her and been taken by her. His unrepentant love of Petal remains, but he is instinctively reaching out to another woman, albeit tentatively. We have a clue to the position of Wavey in the scheme of things when Billy comments that 'Maybe she's the tall and quiet woman' a reference to the saying his old father used. Quoyle does not understand him at this point in the novel, nor may we, though it is to prove most prophetic.

The Tough Baby *is a boat. Yet, as with so many things in this complex and evocative work, we begin to sense layers of meaning, of symbolism working behind the surface detail. Unlike Quoyle's pitiful craft, the* Tough Baby *is virtually unsinkable. Yet despite her appearance of strength, she is destructive and malign. She houses two weak and miserable characters who seem as destructive spiritually as the boat is physically. In contrast to the benign Quoyle, the Melvilles, for all their money and comfort, will remain malicious and bitter, and worse (as we are to find out) – while Quoyle, for all his lowly circumstances, will become increasingly identified in our minds with qualities of spirit that we are invited to approve.*

Chapter 14   WAVEY

Back home, Quoyle tells the aunt that he didn't realise she was in the yacht upholstery business. The aunt tells Quoyle about her shop, and explains how she came into the upholstery business. Her 'significant other', Warren, encouraged her to do a summer course in upholstery. She always dreamed of coming back to the old house with her friend Warren, but when she returned from her course, she discovered that Warren had cancer. Warren had died three months later. The aunt can't explain to Quoyle that getting the puppy and naming her Warren had meant saying the name many times a day to 'invoke the happiness that had been'.

At work, Quoyle thinks of Bunny. He decides to go into town. He gives Wavey a lift. Wavey explains that she works at the school library two days a week. They look at each other's hands and both see gold on the ring finger. She catches him looking at her and flicks her eyes away, 'but both [are] pleased'. Quoyle watches Wavey until she enters the school, entranced.

In telling Quoyle about the loss of her friend 'Warren', the aunt is participating in a process which has already well and truly begun – the mutual revelations, the sharing of fortune and misfortune, the gradual 'knotting' or involvement which binds people together and makes life liveable, the entrusting of secrets. Though the aunt can't explain that Warren, her lover, was a woman, the fact that she is able to tell Quoyle about Warren is a sign of progress.

Also a sign of progress is Quoyle's first direct encounter with Wavey. Almost like a shy schoolboy, he looks to Wavey, and she to him – and '[both are] pleased'. It is the beginning of a relationship which will help mend Quoyle's broken life. With great delicacy, the author shows the bonds that make human existence a pleasure. Note the oblique reference to the 'tall woman' again.

Chapter 15　　　THE UPHOLSTERY SHOP

Quoyle visits the aunt's shop. She introduces Quoyle to her two employees, Mrs Mavis Bangs, and Dawn Budgel. The aunt and Quoyle go to eat at Skipper Will's.

Quoyle asks the aunt about Bunny. He is worried that Bunny is not 'normal' on account of her nightmares and bad tempers. The aunt suggests that Bunny's behaviour is due to a lack of understanding about what has happened. She tries to make Quoyle accept that it's a matter of time, that perhaps Bunny is just more sensitive than other children and can see things beyond everyday reality. Quoyle can't grasp this explanation and fears that Bunny's problems are his fault; 'his own failure to love her enough'. The aunt suggests that it will take time for Bunny to find a way of camouflaging her differences. Quoyle's hand moves up to his chin as the subject is too close to the bone.

In addressing Quoyle's worry about Bunny, the aunt plays a fairly plain mentor role – advising the anxious father not to worry about his daughter, but to trust the passing of time in allowing her to overcome her problems.

Chapter 16　　　BEETY'S KITCHEN

Quoyle picks up his daughters from Dennis and Beety's house. He feels more like a father and has a true sense of family warmth and homeliness at the Buggit's. Sometimes he secretly feels that the Buggits are his parents. He enjoys watching his children playing and sitting in Beety's kitchen, with his girls on his knees, eating freshly baked bread and homemade jam, and listening to Dennis and Beety talk.

Dennis is talking about a mate who has broken his neck, describing him as a marked man, who escaped near death from an octopus attack eight or nine years ago and who has now ended up with a broken neck. He talks about fishing which is in the family's blood. Dennis replies that Jack, his father, has 'the gift', and that's how he knew Jesson was dead. Dennis tells Quoyle that Jack doesn't really run *The Gammy Bird*; Tert Card runs it the way Jack wants it to be run, because Jack would rather be out fishing.

While Dennis is talking, an old man (Skipper Alfred) arrives and Dennis introduces Quoyle. The Skipper describes the Quoyles as a 'savage pack' who nailed men to trees. He says that he's come to see the 'carpenter maid', Bunny, (having heard the story about her climbing up to the roof with the hammer, to help Quoyle). The Skipper gives her a present, a small brass square. Quoyle hopes she hasn't heard what the Skipper said about men nailed to trees.

We should note Quoyle's increasing sense of belonging – the pleasure he takes from feeling 'at home' at Dennis and Beety Buggit's. By now it has become quite clear, in the author's portrait of Killick-Claw, that she is not mocking the small town ways of the Newfoundland people. On the contrary, she evokes the warm sense of community and the bond which they have formed out of necessity against the harsh environment. All is not perfection in Newfoundland, of course, but there is in Proulx's depiction of the people of this rugged island, a great deal of respect and admiration. They are decent, simple, fond people – and they are a major part of Quoyle's rehabilitation. The unexpected arrival of Skipper Alfred with his gift for Bunny is perhaps a reminder of the unexpected connections and generosity of spirit to found in such a community.

Chapter 17 THE SHIPPING NEWS

Quoyle writes the piece on *Tough Baby*, describing how the boat wrought destruction on boats and houses during Hurricane Bob. Quoyle has a 'sense of writing well'. Pleased with his work, he drops the piece proudly onto Tert Card's desk. Card wants to know if Jack asked Quoyle to write the piece. When Card discovers that Quoyle has written the boat profile in place of the car wreck, he intimates that Jack will be furious.

The following day, Card tells Quoyle that Jack wants to see him. Quoyle nervously prepares himself to meet Jack. Expecting the worst, Quoyle tries to explain himself, but Jack doesn't let him finish, as he is very pleased with the feedback Quoyle's article has prompted and tells Quoyle he wants him to write a weekly column on a boat in the harbour: 'The Shipping News'. Jack also promises to order Quoyle a computer. Nutbeem congratulates Quoyle. Quoyle feels 'light and hot': it is the first time in his life that anyone has said he's done something right.

This chapter shows us a major breakthrough. Quoyle, on his own initiative, and allowing his intuitive sense of what allows him to write well, has produced a highly original piece on the Tough Baby. *Tert Card, the arrogant and insecure editor, has anticipated it being the beginning of the end for Quoyle. The very reverse turns out to be the case. Jack, with his own deep, untutored understanding of people and words, recognises that Quoyle has written something well. His congratulation of Quoyle proves that he is not a complete loser. He does have ability. He can make his way. Quoyle's feeling 'light and hot' is the beginning of a blossoming in self-confidence.*

Chapter 18 LOBSTER PIE

Wavey and Herry are in Quoyle's car. Wavey explains to Quoyle that she wants Herry to have a 'decent life', rather than have him hidden away. She is passionate about helping him and tells Quoyle of all that's been done for children in similar situations. She expresses her belief in the possibilities of life. Quoyle drives Wavey to the library on Fridays and Tuesdays and wears his good shirt. He is quite excited.

On the way back, Quoyle stops at Beety's to pick up the girls, and introduces Wavey and Herry. At her house, Wavey invites them in for tea and cakes, but suddenly Bunny spies a white wooden dog amongst the yard sculptures and becomes agitated. Quoyle realises they will have to come for tea another time.

Renovations continue at the old house, and Quoyle hacks away at his secret path towards the ocean. One day Quoyle sees Petal's face in Sunshine's and calls Sunshine to him wanting 'to prolong the quick illusion', but instead, shakes her hand, saying a rhyme that he heard Wavey saying to Herry, 'invoking...that tall woman'.

One Saturday Quoyle goes down to No Name Cove to buy lobsters. The people down there say his boat will drown him one day. Back home, the aunt reels off a list of lobster dishes, making Quoyle's mouth water. The aunt decides on lobster pie. She says that she's invited Dawn for dinner.

Quoyle takes the girls for a ride in the boat. Sunshine wants to go fast, but Bunny grips the edge tightly and howls at the foamy waves in which she imagines yet another white dog.

At dinner time, it emerges that Dawn doesn't eat lobster, because they look like 'big spiders'. Quoyle waits for Bunny's screeching, but it doesn't come, and surprising everyone, she heartily tucks into the pie exclaming that she loves the 'spider meat'.

Dawn reveals to Quoyle that the owners of *Tough Baby* have disappeared without paying her for the upholstery work. The aunt dismisses the subject. She suggests a game of cards and is enthused when Dawn wants to play.

The growing closeness between Quoyle and Wavey is further developed in this chapter. Wavey is no fairy tale heroine. She is a simple woman, not especially beautiful, and with a disabled son. But the warmth of compassion and the ability to care for others emanates from her. In contrast to the abrasive and terminally selfish Petal, whom Quoyle adored for all the wrong reasons, Wavey is revealed to us as a woman capable of deep love, a much more worthy mate. None of this is especially explicit in the narrative, but it certainly comes out in our instinctive response to the character. Yet, we are reminded, Quoyle has not given up Petal. He is between commitments. He wishes to think warmly of Wavey, but has not the courage to throw off his old love first.

The invitation of Dawn to dinner seems to be the aunt playing at match-making. It is significant that Quoyle can only think of Petal when he sees Dawn. The self consciously romantic 'dinner' turns out to be a rather comic disaster, with Dawn rejecting the food especially baked, and Bunny, significantly, against expectation, relishing the 'spider meat'. In passing we might perhaps note that the aunt has suffered a financial setback, as the owners of Tough Baby *have absconded without paying her. Significantly, she has not told Quoyle, keeping this new misfortune close to her, as though she is at pains not to over-burden him.*

Chapter 19   GOOD-BYE BUDDY

Everyone in the office squeezes into Billy's truck to get fish and chips, and to get away from Tert Card for a while. They talk about the paper and the weather. Billy says he can feel the season changing. With a touch of melancholy, he says it's time he went out to attend his father's grave on Gaze Island. Quoyle would like to see the island, so Billy invites him to accompany him on the weekend, weather permitting. Billy reminisces about Killick-Claw before World War Two. He explains that during the War, so much ammunition was dropped at Misky Bay that no-one dares dock there anymore for fear of pulling up a snarl of ammunition with their anchor.

As he talks, a charred vessel being towed by a tug boat comes into view. It is the *Buddy*, from Perdition Cove. From his pocket Quoyle pulls a rough draft of his story about the *Buddy*, accidentally blown up by leaking gas, and reads it aloud.

We are reminded here anew of the disasters beloved of The Gammy Bird. *What are we to make of these disasters, including here a full story about the* Buddy? *Once more we seem to have the theme of a hostile environment, an unkind fate, thrust in our face. The* Gammy Bird*'s salacious mix of 'Blood, Boats and Blowups' is an exaggerated vision of life as a disaster. That we begin to see that not all in life is disastrous, in short that* The Gammy Bird *has a crooked squint in its vision of the world, is a point worth noting.*

Chapter 20   GAZE ISLAND

Quoyle and Billy are heading out to Gaze Island in Billy's skiff. Billy points out named rock formations, which intrigue Quoyle.

Billy asks Quoyle whether he's seen Nolan, the last of the old Quoyles living at the Point. Billy tells him that Nolan is strange, doesn't rely on welfare and so lives very poorly. He warns Quoyle that Nolan believes the old Quoyle house belongs to him. Billy explains that the old Quoyles were 'wild and inbred, half-wits and murderers'. He tells the story about the Quoyle clan dragging the big green house across the ice to the Point during the late nineteenth century.

Quoyle feels a sense of wellbeing out at sea and enjoys listening to Billy talk about all the named rocks and the folklore of Newfoundland. Billy manoeuvres the boat through a narrow passage into the hidden bay of the island. Quoyle is awestruck at the beauty and mystery of this secret and desolate place.

Quoyle follows Billy to the old cemetery. Quoyle thinks about his own father and feels a sense of sadness as he recalls the lack of ceremony surrounding his parents' death. He remembers his father, and all the fruit for which his father had a passion. He recalls blueberry expeditions with his brother and father. He thinks of his father's love for the garden and imagines that he should have been a farmer.

As though he has heard Quoyle's thoughts, Billy says that his father should have been a farmer. While repainting the letters on the grave marker, Billy tells Quoyle the story of how his father came to be on Gaze Island. He was from a boys' home, shipwrecked on his way from England, and taken in by the Prettys. Quoyle asks Billy about his father's expression – the tall and quiet woman. Billy says that his father had told him there are 'four women in every man's heart. The Maid in the Meadow, the Demon Lover, the Stouthearted Woman, the Tall and Quiet Woman'.

The men walk to another cemetery further down the beach, which is overgrown and neglected. Billy yells to Quoyle it is the cemetery of the Quoyles. Billy explains that the Quoyles lured ships onto the rocks. He points to a flat foundation of rocks where the old house had been before it was dragged across the ice to the Point, when the island was gripped by religious fervour which the Quoyles wanted to avoid.

Billy shouts that they have to leave, as a dense fog is moving quickly in across the water. Within minutes they are in the boat, leaving Gaze Island behind and heading back towards Newfoundland.

Let us consider first the inspiring example represented by Billy. The old man has taken Quoyle back to the place of his birth, the wildly beautiful Gaze Island. En route, he talks of the names of the rocks, sings and generally shows himself to be at one with the sea. The sea is not only depicted in this book as a raging tormentor of human beings. Here, it seems benign and welcoming. Billy's father, a man whose own life started in cruelty and hardship and ended in the comforts of a loving family, seems to replicate that same theme being worked out in the story of Quoyle and those around him. Here is the theme of the possibility of human love and bonding, to set against the harshness of tragedy and misfortune.

Quoyle himself feels the stirring of family ties, remembering his own father's attempts, however unsuccessful, at father/son bonding. The theme of family bonds is given a hilarious and disquieting twist when Quoyle is shown the Quoyle cemetery, and learns how wild his ancestors were. Yet, wild or not, they were his people and they belonged here. A sense of belonging is noticeably growing on him.

We also, at last, have the full quotation from Billy's father about women. We begin to see that they approximate to the women in the book. The 'Maid in the meadow' may well represent the innocent daughters of Quoyle (still maids and still in their happy innocence). Petal is unquestionably the 'Demon Lover', seductive but dangerous. We suspect that the 'Stout Hearted Woman' might well be Aunt Agnis. And we have already had several clues to the quiet, cool, trustworthy and reliable 'Tall and Quiet Woman' – Wavey. It would be improper to read into this quaint bit of folklore some sort of cosmic catalogue of all women. But we can see that Quoyle's own experience of women has shown him the variousness of the other sex. Whom should he tend towards? It is increasingly obvious that the Demon Lover was mischievous and broke his heart, and that what he needs perhaps more than anything now is someone reliable and mature. Wavey perfectly fulfils this role.

Chapter 21   POETIC NAVIGATION

As Billy and Quoyle steer towards the rocks, with the fog closing in, he shouts that these are the rocks that the pirate Quoyles lured ships onto. The boat approaches a rock that Billy says is the 'Net-Man'. There is a suitcase caught on it. Quoyle pulls the case into the boat. He cannot see anything through the dense fog, but somehow Billy manages to steer the right course and both are relieved when they reach the 'Home Rock'.

Finally ashore, they realise that the suitcase is giving off a horrid stench. Quoyle can't stop thinking about opening the suitcase to find out what's inside. Billy hopes it's packed with treasure. Quoyle breaks the lock. Under the dim wharf light he sees the flattened and ruined face of Bayonet Melville lying on a bed of seaweed.

The sea may be benign at times, but can also be dangerous. There is more than a hint of danger in Billy and Quoyle's fog-bound return to Newfoundland. All the quaint rock names in the world cannot disguise the fact that they are in physical danger.

As if to reinforce the dark side of existence in positively ghoulish form, the discovery by Quoyle of Melville's severed head, the comic end of the chapter, is there as a reminder.

Chapter 22   DOGS AND CATS

Mavis talks with Dawn about whether Mrs Melville was responsible for decapitating her husband. Dawn keeps typing her job applications. She will do anything to get away from water, fishing boats, the sound of Mavis prattling on, and the mundanity of Newfoundland in general. Mavis and Dawn agree that 'nothing good ever happened with a Quoyle'.

Quoyle and Wavey sit side by side driving towards her house. A man is there. He is Wavey's brother, Ken. The brother has heard the news about Quoyle finding the severed head and mentions that his dad has seen the new roof on the house, through his telescope. Quoyle feels happy. Ken gets a lift with Quoyle. He invites Quoyle to come and see Wavey whenever he likes.

Lest we rhapsodise too much on the subject of quaint, small town life, Proulx reminds us here that not everyone adores Killock-Claw. Dawn cannot wait to get out of the place. The virtues of small town life are well and truly underlined in Proulx's largely celebratory account of families like the Buggits, but the author is not simple-minded enough to suggest that simply retiring to a small seaside port is the cure for everyone's problems.

Chapter 23   MALEFICIUM

Even though the house is freshly painted and repaired, Quoyle thinks it looks raw and ugly. The aunt's enthusiasm for renovations is waning and she spends more time in her room, staring at the ceiling.

The aunt notices someone coming down the road. Quoyle knows it's the old man Billy told him about. The aunt is reluctant to hear about the old relative.

Before dawn Quoyle wakes and sees a torch beam flash across the ceiling of his room. Quoyle suggests that they pay the old relative a visit, but the aunt is reluctant. Quoyle doesn't mention the torch beam, but tries to coax her into taking a trip to the deserted village at Capsize Cove. The aunt declines.

As if to make a similar contrary case (to that about small town life) about family, this chapter, significantly entitled Maleficium (bad deeds), presents us with the half mad Quoyle who is harrassing his young relative. The aunt does not want to meet the old man, and we will in due course find out why. In the meantime, Nolan is a reminder that family, while usually nurturant and supportive, can be a malicious and disturbing thing as well.

Chapter 24   BERRY PICKING

On the first day of school, Bunny is afraid, but she refuses Quoyle's offer to go with her and joins the crowd, looking for her friend, Marty Buggit. At the end of the school day, Quoyle is waiting for Bunny, expecting her to have had a miserable day, but she has had fun. She proudly shows him a piece of paper on which she has scrawled her name.

The aunt suggests inviting Wavey berry picking. Wavey delightedly accepts the invitation. Ken brings her over. Armed with buckets, Quoyle, the aunt, Wavey, Herry and the girls set out to pick berries. Wavey and Quoyle pick near each other. Reminded by the aunt that they've forgotten the picnic basket, Quoyle sets back to get it, asking Wavey to come.

While Wavey is standing on a rock, looking out to sea, Quoyle clasps his hands around her ankles, and presses his face against her stockinged legs. Wavey, uncomfortable with the physical contact, recalls her dead husband, lost at sea. Wavey says she always thinks of Herold when she's by the sea, even though years have passed since he was drowned.

On their way back to the others, however, Wavey stops suddenly and turns to Quoyle, and they end up rolling over berry plants in a tangle of 'mouths and tears and stupid words', until Wavey pulls away, running towards the aunt and the children. Quoyle stares as Wavey runs and presses himself against the earth as though at one with nature. He is filled with a deep sense of understanding and overwhelmed with a feeling of contentment and the realisation that everything will fulfil its destiny with the passing of time. Quoyle senses the possibilities inherent in everything surrounding him.

Against Quoyle's expectations that school will be another disaster for the child he has pigeon-holed as a difficult if not hysterical individual (not unlike himself in many ways), Bunny in fact turns out to enjoy school very much. We are given a little jolt, effectively, as we realise that Quoyle's pessimistic expectations are not necessarily fulfilled.

The picnic scene is of course enormously important. Let us start by noting the wonderfully positive atmosphere of the whole scene – the early autumn day, warm, sunny, with the sea in a benign mood, the aunt and children happily picking berries. Life can be good. Much more obvious than these tonal aspects however is the physical encounter between Quoyle and Wavey. The scene where Quoyle embraces Wavey's legs is one of powerful eroticism – all the more so in that it doesn't involve either character being unclothed. The coming together of man and woman is described with marvellous power and discretion. That Wavey clearly feels guilty at the relationship proceeding too fast, and that she pulls back at first from Quoyle's embrace, is perhaps a necessary reminder that she, unlike Petal, is not fast or loose with her affections. Her loyalty to her dead husband is not silly, we must remind ourselves, but a laudable quality. The comic reversal of this feigned standoffishness in the wonderful scene where they roll on the grass, funny and moving at the same time, is of course a sign that the two have made a move forward.

By the end of the chapter, as Quoyle lies on the grass, feeling at one with life, we know that the balance has shifted in his view of the human condition. The vision he has at this moment is almost an ecstatic one. The past is 'rinsed of evil', the future becomes a sweet one (in his mind, he and Wavey will marry and all will be well) and all of life comes before his eyes into a 'trembling balance'. This moment of epiphany (insight or revelation) is a vital one in the narrative. When we read that in Quoyle's view, 'All the complex wires of life were stripped out and he could see the structure of life .... that tiny figures of humans and animals against [rock and sea] for a brief time,' we suspect we are seeing the nature of human life itself, beautiful but transitory, against the background of what little time we have. It is a very beautiful scene, and for a book which often seems somewhat bleak, is a moment of pure joy in the miracle of life.

Chapter 25   OIL

Quoyle stops at an eatery for toast and tea on his way to the office. Tert Card and Billy are there too. Card is insisting that the future of Newfoundland is in oil. He reels off the virtues of progress while Billy and a fisheries plant man argue about the ills of modern society: crime, materialism, drugs, pollution, deforestation, reduction of fish numbers and so on.

Back at the office, Quoyle hands Card his article illustrating the ugliness of oil tankers and the pollution they cause. Later, Card avenges himself by rewriting the piece, changing the angle in support of economic progress and the beauty of tankers and, having done so, goes out to get drunk.

The next morning Quoyle confronts Card about the alteration of his column. Quoyle is angry that Card has made him sound like a 'mouthpiece for tanker interests'. By confronting Card, Quoyle has surprised Billy and Nutbeem as well as himself. Although Quoyle wants to call Jack immediately to sort out the situation, Nutbeem advises him not to disturb Jack at home. He promises to talk to Jack about it himself.

Jack calls the office the following day. He wants Quoyle to keep writing his column, without interference from Card, and to permanently cover boat wrecks, of which there are plenty, to use during the weeks when there are no car wrecks.

In what amounts to the continuing debate about the nature of places like Newfoundland, we have in this chapter the debate, or battle, between Tert Card, representing the 'new' Newfoundland, devoted to materialism and 'Progress', while Billy and Quoyle on the other hand represent the idea of the old ways and the old virtues. We are, without doubt, invited to side with Billy and Quoyle, far more sympathetic characters than Card. This battle takes an amusing turn when Card thinks he has subverted Quoyle's view of progress with his own rewrite, only to find his rewrite panned by the boss. Might we detect the author's opinions speaking through this twist?

Chapter 26   DEADMAN

For the first time, Quoyle is alone in the old house. He enjoys his time alone, cooking his favourite meals, walking down to the dock at twilight. Once his article is written,

Quoyle decides to take a walk to the end of the Point. As he pulls the door shut, from the knob falls a piece of knotted string, which he puts in his pocket.

The Point seems like 'the end of the world' to Quoyle, and he is excited by its violent beauty, its raw energy. He thinks of all those who have sailed these rough waters throughout history. Looking down, he sees a human figure in a yellow suit, trapped in a cave, its head under the surface of the water.

Quoyle needs to tell someone about the body. He decides his boat will be faster than a car. Inexperience prevents Quoyle from setting a zigzag course across the rough sea and his boat pitches in the swell. Suddenly it capsizes and Quoyle is thrown underwater. Terrified, he manages to pull himself to the upturned boat. He flips it over, but it refills and he is plunged down once again. He sees the boat sink below him. An empty esky he had in the boat floats nearby and Quoyle manages to cling onto it. Hours pass. After a time, he cannot feel his legs. He thinks it ironic that he might end up companion to the dead man in yellow. Delirious, Quoyle welcomes the thought of sleep. Suddenly though, Jack Buggit appears, swearing and pulling him out of the water, saying he had felt someone was in danger.

In Mrs Buggit's kitchen, Quoyle is warmed with hot water bottles, blankets and steaming mugs of tea. Mrs Buggit comments on how many Jack has saved from drowning. She says Quoyle's heavy build was responsible for keeping him alive.

Finally Quoyle remembers the man in yellow and retells his story. With the Coast Guard, Billy Pretty and Tert Card informed about the yellow man, Mrs Buggit sets Quoyle up in the guest room. She advises him to have his next boat made by Alvin Yark. The following morning Quoyle is ravenous and 'euphoric with life'.

The dark side of life reappears with a vengeance in this chapter. The first intimation is Quoyle's discovery of the dead body in the water. This is followed swiftly by his own close encounter with an icy death. It is interesting to reflect on the fact that by this stage of the book, our identification with Quoyle has intensified to the point where we feel his near drowning would be a terrible thing. The pathetic thoughts he has as he believes he awaits a certain death underline for us how precious he has become. Ugly and clumsy he may be, a misfit and something of a joke even, he is nonetheless delineated in our minds as a warm human being, whose loss would be a tragedy.

That he is rescued by the old man of the sea, his boss Jack, at which point the drama turns into both relief and comedy, links in with other stories of Jack's 'second sight' and his intimate relationship with the sea. The sea may have been about to take Quoyle, but someone who knows the ways of the sea, who knows how to survive, is his rescuer. Quoyle, by now our reluctant hero, will go on to further adventures. Note that his rescue leaves Quoyle 'euphoric [ecstatic] with life'. If one thing could be said for encounters with death, it is that they reinforce the deep joy of being alive.

Chapter 27   NEWSROOM

Two days after Quoyle's ordeal, Billy Pretty comes in with news of the dead man. It is thought to be the decapitated Mr Melville, whose body had been inserted into the suit in five separate pieces. Pretty begins to type out a page one story on the dramatic find.

Nutbeem complains that he never gets any good stories, only sordid ones. He runs through all his stories for the week and Quoyle is astonished at the number of them. Card says they're what sell the paper. Quoyle tells him about his profile of an old fisherman whose boat sank a day after he placed an advertisement for it in *The Gammy Bird*. Quoyle rereads a letter from Partridge telling of his high life, all the things he and Mercalia have bought, and inviting Quoyle to visit any time.

At Skipper Will's, Nutbeem mentions Jack's 'uncanny sense about assignments'. Quoyle's wife was killed in a car accident, and he is assigned the car wreck stories. Billy covers the home news when he has never married. Nutbeem himself was assaulted for three years during his childhood, and he is assigned the sexual abuse stories. Quoyle sees a parallel with what Jack does to himself: spending most of his time at sea when it has claimed several members of his family. Quoyle realises that confronting these fears allows them to dissipate, through the recognition that one's fate is not unique, 'that other people suffer as you suffer'.

Quoyle enjoys his daily routine, taking Sunshine to Beety's in the morning, dropping Bunny at school and giving Wavey a lift. This routine is reversed in the afternoons, when Quoyle especially enjoys having tea at Wavey's. She cuts his hair, and looks after the children when he works late. In return he cuts her wood on the weekends, and drives her places. Their lives begin to grow closer together. Quoyle admires her brightly painted souvenirs, (sold on consignment at gift shops along the coast), and the colourful furniture, meticulously painted, which Quoyle interprets as an expression of her inner passion and vibrance.

With Nutbeem and Quoyle's conversation about The Gammy Bird, *we finally see something of a profound wisdom on the part of Jack. Nutbeem articulates it very well when he points out that Jack has an 'uncanny sense' about what jobs he gives the various writers. Each one is forced to confront his own worst fear. As Nutbeem says, perhaps there is a therapeutic quality to this in that 'pain is supposed to ease and dull through repetetive confrontation' and that 'you see your condition is not unique, that other people suffer as you suffer'. What is happening to the men at* The Gammy Bird *is, in a way, what Proulx hints happens in life as a whole – we are bound to other people partly by pleasure and friendship, and partly by a shared sense of our common pain at the inevitable hardships and traumas life brings us.* The Gammy Bird *mirrors life. We learn to be more humane and to treasure what we have more by confronting the things which can take away pleasure and even life itself.*

Chapter 28   THE SKATER'S CHAIN GRIP

To get away from Quoyle and his children, the aunt goes out to the Point. She comes across an iced-over pond and remembers it from her childhood. She recalls herself at the age of eleven or twelve, skating alone on this same pond and the man who sexually accosted her. Memories of harsh winters in the old house flood her mind. These thoughts make her shudder, but she acknowledges that she was hardened by those experiences; they forced her to become stronger and accept her lot in life.

Back home, she talks about the forthcoming winter and wonders how they will manage with the road snowed over. She expresses her desire to be closer to town; to be able to see a movie and eat at a restaurant, and admits that winter scares her. Quoyle suggests renting a house during the winter months.

At the shop, Mrs Bangs suggests buying the house belonging to the Burkes. The aunt is reluctant, having already spent much money on the old house. She looks through her mail. Amongst the correspondence is a package from Macau. She tears it open to find a wad of American money tied with a blue cord. The aunt sees that it is a strip of blue leather, the colour of the Melville's upholstery.

Another pithy reminder of one of the author's themes appears here as the aunt's recollection of her childhood encounter on the frozen pond. The man who sexually abused her (the first, as we later find out, of two such people) threatened her in a most profound way. She is perfectly normal in shuddering at the memory of the experience, and other aspects of her childhood. There is however an upside to such difficult material: 'life had hardened her, she had made her own way along the rough coasts, had patched and mended her sails, replaced chafed gear with strong, fit stuff. She had worked her way off the rocks and shoals. Had managed. Still managed.' We cannot miss the metaphoric quality of this passage. She learnt to survive, to endure – and this is something to admire.

Chapter 29   ALVIN YARK

Quoyle and his girls are in Beety's kitchen, when Tert Card walks in, and announces that Quoyle should ring Diddy Shovel about a ship fire. Before Quoyle can call, the phone rings for him. It's Billy, inquiring whether Quoyle has seen Alvin Yark yet about a boat. He advises Quoyle that winter is the best time to have a boat made and that it's essential he get back to boats on account of his bad experience. Billy offers to take Quoyle out to sea once the ice disperses, to teach him the ropes.

Quoyle rings Diddy Shovel to hear that a huge cargo vessel, carrying zinc and lead powder, is aflame. Diddy tells Quoyle the ship should be in the dock by five.

Quoyle picks up Wavey. Quoyle senses the unfolding of something between them. He does not think his growing feelings towards her are the first signs of love, for he believes that love involves suffering, and besides, he thinks love only comes once a lifetime. He picks up Bunny from school. As they drive, Quoyle mentions going to Alvin Yark's on Saturday to discuss plans for a boat. Wavey is delighted at this. (Alvin is her uncle.) She suggests that they all go together and have supper there. Quoyle heads for the dock, but they arrive to find that the cargo ship has been taken to another dock along the coast.

On Saturday, Quoyle, Wavey and the children head through the dense fog to the Yark's house. Mrs Yark offers tea and biscuits. Quoyle leaves the women in the kitchen to join Alvin in his dim workshop. Alvin advises Quoyle on a suitable boat, but explains that it will probably take until spring to build.

What are we to make of Alvin Yark? Is he merely a comic book yokel, a funny old figure speaking mutilated English and fussing away over his boats in his dark shed?

Perhaps he is an amusing character, but we are not invited to mock him. As with other of her quaint old characters, so too Yark is offered to us sincerely enough as a representative of a vanishing breed – the old time craftsman, proud of his work, humble in his modest achievements of skill and creativity. There is a sweet atmosphere to the scene where Quoyle watches the old man work, and knows that he is in touch, through his hands and the boats he creates, strong, seaworthy boats, with the natural world and the people his work protects.

Chapter 30   THE SUN CLOUDED OVER

Quoyle, Bunny and Sunshine meet the aunt at a restaurant. The aunt, looking a little fragile, says that she has missed them. Quoyle laughs; they have missed her too. Bunny and Sunshine chatter about what they want for Christmas.

The aunt announces that she has changed her business name to Hamm's Maritime Upholstery and has got a big job reupholstering the cargo vessel which caught fire. The job entails spending the winter in the coastal town of St. John's. Mrs Bangs and Dawn will accompany her. The aunt says they can move out to the old house in spring, as long as Quoyle hasn't considered moving back to New York. Quoyle has no intention of leaving Newfoundland.

Bunny is trying to give a demonstration of something Skipper Alfred showed her with a bit of string. Bunny pulls and loops the string into several shapes. Quoyle is impressed.

Note how the aunt acknowledges her reunion with Quoyle and his daughters: she has missed them. It is a simple enough comment, an everyday remark. But this comes from a woman who has been through traumas in her life, whose bond with the Quoyle family was effectively severed for years, and who only by accident joined up with her nephew and his children again. That she has missed them indicates that they have become part of her life. The aunt too has changed, and knotted her fortunes together with other people.

When, at the end of this chapter, Bunny shows her ability to do a cat's cradle design with string, we are reminded of the positive sense in which knots can be taken. The book sets up the idea of knots in several senses, but here we see it in its positive connotation – of binding, joining, making something worthwhile and complete. It is a metaphor for the growing closeness of the Quoyle family.

Chapter 31   SOMETIMES YOU JUST LOSE IT

Quoyle writes of a ship collision with a cliff. Tert Card enters the office complaining about the icy weather. He says it's no wonder so many people in Newfoundland deliberately slide off the cliff roads at this time of year. He reminisces about travel to a warmer place with palm trees and the scent of suntan oil. Nutbeem says he's going to remember Newfoundland for many things. He is excited about heading off in his sailing boat again, out of the snow towards 'adventure and love'. Billy Pretty adds that it's the time of year that people leave Newfoundland, although he is amongst the few who have remained over the years. He wonders whether Quoyle will be the next to leave, though Quoyle assures them all that he's staying, considering Alvin Yark is building him a boat, Bunny is succeeding at school, Sunshine loves being at Beety's, and the aunt will be back in spring. He adds that all they need is a place to live.

By the time Nutbeem decides he is leaving Newfoundland, Quoyle has been there some time. He arrived before the summer and now winter is approaching. Nutbeem asks Quoyle if he will be leaving, and Quoyle, in what is a most revealing reply, tells him that he is now having a boat built, Bunny is succeeding, Sunshine is happy, and in effect, although he has no house to live in, he calls the place home. It is a most significant admission, betokening much about Quoyle's development.

Chapter 32   THE HAIRY DEVIL

On the day of Nutbeem's farewell party, Quoyle picks Bunny up from school and takes her to Beety's. Sunshine divulges a secret that Beety is teaching her how to knit and she is making Quoyle a Christmas present. The feeling in the Buggit's household is one of warmth and affection.

Quoyle and Nutbeem arrive at Nutbeem's trailer with a car load of alcohol and food. Soon the trailer is crowded with noisy, drunken men. Quoyle begins to enjoy himself in the unfamiliar environment. Card tells a story about a friend of his father's who one night strayed from their camp and disappeared into a hole in the snow. His father investigated the hole in the morning, felt something behind him and turned to see a 'hairy devil' jumping into the hole, saying he'd be back for his father once he'd done his dishes. Card says his father ran for miles. Drunkenly, Quoyle responds to Card by bawling that his wife is dead.

The party is becoming violent. Twenty drunk men hoist the trailer off its blocks at one end, and fights break out. As the mayhem increases, Quoyle hears the men reverting to a local dialect which he doesn't understand. He watches as a black-haired man picks up an axe from Nutbeem's woodpile and shouts to the men to axe Nutbeem's boat, to prevent him from leaving. Nutbeem screams to the men to leave his boat alone, but they are already rushing away. Armed with chainsaws, sticks and rocks, the men attack Nutbeem's newly repaired boat, stocked with provisions for his journey. To a chant begun by the dark-haired man (about how they love Nutbeem), the men wildly attack the boat until it sinks.

Unaware of these occurrences, Quoyle walks back towards Killick-Claw. He walks to Wavey's house and watches, unobserved, from outside her kitchen window as Herry dances to her accordion playing. Forgetting his bed in Dennis and Beety's basement, Quoyle rents a room at the inn.

How are we to take the party at Nutbeem's trailer? Does this turn on its head all the positive attributes of Newfoundlanders we have been invited to consider? Have they suddenly become animals and brutes? No. Although the party is appalling in its violence, drunkeness and the destruction which is later visited upon poor Nutbeem's boat, and while the author is not concealing from us the excesses to which these men may be led when under the influence of alcohol, she is not suggesting that we reverse our perception. In a kind of black comedy, we see them at their worst. Yet even their drunken destruction of Nutbeem's beloved boat is ostensibly to keep Nutbeem with them – small comfort to him, but a sign of bonding and community nonetheless.

Chapter 33   THE COUSIN

In the morning, Quoyle is hung over. He recalls Nutbeem's trailer being pulled off its foundations. He tries to call Nutbeem but there is no answer.

Arriving in a taxi at Nutbeem's, Quoyle sees the sagging trailer with a mess of bottles in the yard. He decides he doesn't want to live in the trailer. There is no sign of Nutbeem. At Dennis and Beety's, Quoyle finds out about the destruction of Nutbeem's boat. The children have colds and although Quoyle was planning to take them out to the house with him, to give Beety a break, she suggests they remain with her for the day. She says they're like her own children. Quoyle thanks Beety for being 'all the help in the world' and mentions that he saw Dennis and Jack together at the party. Beety says that gossip spread the rumour that they didn't speak to one another. He tells Beety he doesn't want to live in the trailer and she suggests approaching the Burkes, as they haven't yet sold their house.

The road to Quoyle's Point seems miserable. Quoyle acknowledges his love for the coast, but the house itself seems wrong to him. He doesn't feel bound to it like the aunt. As he looks around the house Quoyle sees that someone has placed knotted string at the entrance to each room. Enraged, Quoyle collects the strings in his pockets and heads towards Capsize Cove, with the idea of confronting the cousin and putting an end to the rivalry.

He knocks on the door of a building from which smoke is rising. Seeing Nolan, Quoyle is alarmed at the family resemblances evident in the cousin's haggard face. The man has a white dog. Quoyle pulls out the knotted strings and drops them to the floor. The cousin snatches them and throws them into the stove, saying that the knots are now fixed by fire and will never undo. Despite the fear instilled in Bunny by the white dog and the knots, Quoyle cannot bring himself to shout at the old man. He pities Nolan and his pathetic attempts to defend himself from 'imagined enemies' with knots in string.

Alvin Yark is working on a piece of timber for Quoyle's boat. Quoyle helps lift and haul. As he works, Yark intermittently breaks into song, as well as telling Quoyle the story of an uncle who built his own coffin in the shape of a boat, complete with a motor, to carry him out to sea. The skeleton of Quoyle's boat is completed.

Nutbeem, Dennis, Billy Pretty and the black-haired man are sitting on the steps of Nutbeem's trailer drinking beer when Quoyle arrives. Nutbeem says he probably wouldn't have made it anyway and that he's changed his plans; he has decided to fly to the warmth of Brazil. He adds that the landlords have decided not to rent the trailer out to a newspaper man again. Quoyle is silently relieved.

Back at the house at Quoyle's Point, Quoyle finds the knot curses left by his unfortunate cousin, old Nolan. This leads to the long postponed confrontation with the mad

old man. At long last we see, of course, that Bunny was not imagining the white dog –
it was a real animal, the old man's ghostly companion. Nor was Quoyle imagining the
knots – they were the other side of the bondage of family, the twisted, vengeful result of
the old man's jealousy about the younger Quoyle and his apparently good life. Quoyle,
quite rightly, does not take out his anger on the old man, though clearly he has both
strength and justice on his side. He sees that the old man is in fact a pathetic relic of a
bygone age, more to be pitied than condemned. A point is being made here too. Quoyle
may not be a romantic hero, or glamourous, but he possesses the qualities we should
admire – compassion, a growing wisdom, and the ability to deal with adversity in a
strong but measured way.

Chapter 34   DRESSING UP

Tert Card offers to buy Quoyle a drink at a nearby pub. Card is leaving for St. John's
on New Year's Day, having accepted a position there to set up a newsletter for the oil
riggers. Quoyle leaves, saying he's going to pick up his children.

Bunny talks about the school pageant. Quoyle doesn't like Christmas, with its
frenzied shopping and debt. He remembers a time when his brother received a set of
Matchbox cars. Quoyle remembers only ever receiving pyjamas or shirts which his
mother bought because he grew so fast.

At the pageant everyone is in their very best clothes, and the hall is abuzz with
excitement. Quoyle is surprised to find that members of the community perform too,
not just school children. Bunny and her best friend Marty sing a song. Quoyle is pleased.
Wavey and Herry come on stage. Herry is wearing a sailor suit and tap shoes, and the
whole audience claps and shouts to the accordian and dancing. Beety, in a cabaret
style outfit, enacts a hilarious skit about Billy Pretty and a couple of local identities.
Dennis is awfully proud of his wife.

For Christmas, Quoyle gives Wavey a teapot and a silk scarf and she gives him
a handknitted jumper of the perfect size. The only thing Petal ever gave him is vivid in
his mind (two eggs). Quoyle spends Christmas day at the Buggit's, with the aunt, who
is back from St. John's.

The following morning, Dennis suggests they go and check on Nolan. They go
by boat to Capsize Cove. Both dog and man are barely alive. Dennis gives the old man
a loaf of bread and watches as he eats it. Dennis says to Quoyle that the man needs to
go into a home as he's starving and half mad. Dennis says he'll drown the half dead
dog, but the old man, being Quoyle's kin, is *his* responsibility. Dennis says Beety and
Wavey will know of a nursing home. Dennis explains how Beety and Wavey set up an
establishment that helps women in dire circumstances. Quoyle's guilt is heightened.
He thinks he should have done something the first time he visited the old man.

The Christmas Pageant is another of the now quite common scenes of communal festivity
with which Proulx provides us from time to time. The performance, rustic and unso-
phisticated though it may be, is full of a simple joy. The joke about Billy and the old
lady, the heartwarming sight of Wavey and Herry performing, the powerful sense of
communal bonding, all emerge forcefully but subtly in this episode. Here is another of

the reasons Quoyle is 'getting better' – he is surrounded by people whose simple values and unselfconscious togetherness is part of what makes their lives worthwhile.

The renewed visit to old Nolan is confronting. Although Dennis is the one who speaks the words, Quoyle is the one who accepts the responsibility. Foul as he may be, Nolan is kin. Quoyle knows that he must do something about the old man. He has accepted his place in the knotted fretwork of family. It is a significant point.

Chapter 35   THE DAY'S WORK

Jack announces that Billy Pretty wants to continue writing the home pages, so he is assigning Quoyle as editor to replace Tert Card. He adds that he wants Quoyle to continue writing the shipping news. Jack explains he'll try Benny Fudge on the car wrecks and sexual abuse stories. Jack asks Quoyle's opinion on changing the home pages. He wants to focus on lifestyles. Quoyle suggests a column in the form of a letter, from people who have left Newfoundland. Jack asks whether Quoyle can handle his newly assigned position and Quoyle nods and vows to himself that there will 'never be a typo'.

When the first paper comes out with Quoyle's name as editor, he tears out the masthead and sends it to his friend Partridge. When he discovers the news about Mrs Melville, siezed in Hawaii, with a young steward from the boat, he sends a copy to his aunt.

Another milestone is presented to us in this chapter. With Tert Card going, Quoyle will become the new editor of The Gammy Bird. It may be a surprise to Quoyle, but perhaps it is not so for the reader. Quoyle's real abilities have finally been recognised. Quoyle's natural pleasure in being awarded the job is not ambition fulfilled, or any material gain, but his recognition of how far he has come – from being a failed hack journalist to being managing editor of a newspaper. What it says about his developing self-confidence is immeasurable.

Chapter 36   STRAIT JACKET

Partridge rings, telling Quoyle that a maniac went into the *Mockingburg Record* office with a machine gun and killed Ed Punch, Al Catalog and four others. The cause was a letter to the editor about the necessity of riots which had been deemed unsuitable to print. Partridge says that Mercalia was shot at while driving her truck and she narrowly escaped being killed. Partridge says it's a crazy place.

Down at the dock, Quoyle tells Jack the news about the shooting in Mockingburg. Jack replies that things aren't that bad in Newfoundland. Jack explains his reasons for fishing. He reminisces about the 'old days'. Jack is disgusted that they have to live by rules made by people who have never set foot in Newfoundland, but Quoyle doesn't see this as strange; rather, he thinks Jack lucky that he's only just begun to feel the effects of such a common political situation.

Papers arrive for Quoyle to sign his old cousin into care for the rest of his life. Quoyle decides he will visit the old man in St. John's before he signs his life away. He invites Wavey to come with him, suggesting dinner and a movie. Wavey agrees, saying that Herry can stay with his grandfather. The car trip to St. John's begins in silence, but slowly both Quoyle and Wavey begin to grow comfortable with conversation.

In town, Wavey takes great pleasure in buying clothes for Bunny and Sunshine with the list and money Quoyle has given her. Quoyle scouts the mental institution's gift shop, wanting to take something to Nolan, but cannot think of what to buy a man whose life he knows little about. He decides on a photo frame with a poodle picture inside it.

Quoyle sits down with the old man, who talks about the food, showers, clean clothes and games, and that the 'place is full of loonies'. He tells Quoyle that he pretends to be mad too so that he can continue to receive the good food and luxurious treatment. Quoyle pulls the photo frame from his pocket. Holding it in one hand, Nolan looks out to sea and painfully speaks about the knots he tied against Quoyle, the winds he summoned. He thinks about the dead sheep and the dog, Whiteface. Quoyle consoles him, saying that is all past. Quoyle says he will endeavour to get the old man into the home in Killick-Claw. The old man replies that he never wanted to be in Capsize Cove anyway; it was circumstance that drove him there because, like all the Quoyles, he had no luck.

Nolan asks Quoyle where Agnis is and says that she has never come to see him. Nolan says it is because the aunt is ashamed of what he knows. He explains that when Agnis was a girl, she came to his house in tears to see his wife for 'women's dirty business'. He saw 'something bloody in the basin' and knew that the aunt's brother, Quoyle's father, had been responsible for her pregnancy. Quoyle is shocked.

At night, Quoyle forgets about the old cousin and enjoys Wavey's company. Over dinner, Quoyle and Wavey look at one another, 'briefly at first, then with prolonged and piercing gazes'. After dinner Quoyle and Wavey see a movie, and then retire to bed together. In Quoyle's arms, Wavey says that the hotel is the same one where she spent her honeymoon with Herold.

Quoyle's visit to the institution the following morning brings the discovery that the old man can't have any visitors as he had broken the photo frame's glass and had tried to stab all those who came near. The 'Golden Age Home' Quoyle had suggested is no possibility now.

As if to reinforce the contrast being proposed by the author between the emptiness and occasional violence of urban life, and the relative security and authenticity of small town life, comes the news from Partridge. These events could not happen in Killick-Claw, we surmise. In the same vein somewhat are Jack's reminiscences about 'the good old days'. Times are changing, and the simple and pleasurable, if rugged, lifestyle Jack clings to is gradually fading away. Proulx is not suggesting that the old fishing life was without its hardships, or perfect, but she does seem to be making an argument that the simple life of people living in a close community in harmony with nature was, for all its occasional tragedies, a good life.

The trip that Quoyle and Wavey take to visit old Nolan is a significant one. What Quoyle learns from Nolan about Agnis' childhood, the incestuous relationship with the brother (his father), perhaps an explanation of why she went the way she did in her own relationship, seems a recapitulation of the ghosts of sins past theme – the old pirate Quoyles thread in the book.

In the final physical union of Quoyle and Wavey, we have something much more positive. The aunt may have been brutilised by her relationships with men, but Wavey does not suffer at the hands of Quoyle. On the contrary, she finds comfort and happiness. The simple, almost naive romance of dinner and their sleeping together casts a warm glow. The two are connected intimately now, and though Quoyle may have difficulty equating what he experiences with Wavey with love, there is no doubt in the reader's mind that the relationship is a wholesome and life-affirming one.

Chapter 37   SLINGSTONES

Back at *The Gammy Bird*, Quoyle discovers that Bunny has pushed one of the teachers. The principal urges him to come immediately to the school. Bunny is seated outside the principal's office with her face set into a defiant look. The principal informs Quoyle that she will have to suspend Bunny until she explains her actions and apologises to the teacher. Quoyle takes her away. Bunny doesn't divulge much, but the story emerges indirectly. Bunny had stood up for Herry Prowse, humiliated by the fill-in teacher. Quoyle tells the aunt, who insists on catching an early plane to be with them when they see the principal the following day. The aunt speaks hotly, but it is Quoyle who finally explains and coaxes and smoothes things out, arranging apologies.

A routine has emerged in Quoyle's life. On Saturdays, he, Wavey, and the children go to the Yark's. In the car Wavey looks at Bunny, communicates without words and takes her hand in hers. Everyone feels a sense of harmony. In the Yark's kitchen, Wavey and her aunt Evvie work at a hooked rug, Bunny reads a picture book and Sunshine and Herry play. Bunny suddenly mentions Petal, saying that she was in a car accident in New York and she can't wake up, but when she is grown up she might go there and wake her up.

In his workshop, Alvin Yark works on Quoyle's boat. Yark asks when Quoyle and Wavey are 'to do the deed'. Quoyle answers that he doesn't know. The memory of Petal is still strong, and Wavey is always thinking about Herold. Yark tells Quoyle that Herold had made Wavey's life miserable, as he'd had affairs and children all along the coast. He says that some had breathed a sigh of relief when Herold disappeared.

One day, Wavey appears with seal flipper pie for Quoyle. Quoyle leaves the hot pie on the table while he drives Wavey home. At night while Quoyle is licking the last of the pie out of the dish, Wavey comes through the kitchen door, and says that Herry is sleeping at her dad's and she is sleeping here with Quoyle.

A few days later Quoyle is telling Wavey about Petal, the eggs she gave him and how she hated cooking. He recalls all the dinners he cooked and all the meals he ate with the children while Petal was out with her boyfriends. Wavey is shocked to hear about Petal's affairs, and tells Quoyle about Herold's behaviour. The two confide in each other, secrets they have never spoken, and it brings them a certain comfort to have shared their similar experiences of unrequited love.

Quoyle, Wavey and the children are having a picnic by the sea. Sunshine calls to Wavey to ask whether she has brought marshmallows. Wavey calls her 'maid' and

Quoyle thinks of the 'Maids of the Meadow'. The significance of Billy's father's verse to Quoyle's life becomes apparent. Quoyle's girls call out 'Dad' repeatedly, asking when the food will be ready and Herry says 'Dad' too, grinning.

A couple of weeks later, Billy, Quoyle and Dennis help Jack with his lobster pots. Jack has a pile of stones ('slingstones') in the corner of his shack which serve as anchors for the lobster pots. Billy says its a shame they don't have cause to celebrate, but Quoyle says they do because the aunt's coming back and he's throwing a party.

The episode involving Bunny offers a lovely surprise. Our first inclination is to see this new 'misbehaviour' of Bunny as another sign that she is a disturbed child. The reverse turns out to be the case, happily. Her 'misbehaviour' was a result of her wish to defend Herry. Bunny has grown up a little too, learnt compassion (obviously from those around her) and her action, far from being a sign of disturbance, is a sign of mental and emotional good health. It also suggests the strength of the knot or bond which has formed between the Quoyles and Wavey and her unfortunate son. This latter is reinforced strongly, if silently, in the scene in the Yark kitchen.

What Alvin reveals about Herold Prowse is set up in our mind immediately as a fascinating parallel. Wavey too was abused by her spouse. She suffered the infidelities of a brutal husband, just as Quoyle suffered the infidelities of a heartless wife. The author is not playing gender favourites on this one, not suggesting that either sex has a monopoly on virtue or vice. Quoyle and Wavey are both damaged people, with burdened pasts, their earlier experience of love a cruel one. We are not being invited to see Wavey and Quoyle as clinging to one another as victims. It is far more positive a thing than that. Certainly they are reaching out to one another for physical and emotional comfort, but this is not, increasingly, love on the rebound – it is the real thing. When Wavey comes of her own accord to sleep with Quoyle we see that their bond with one another has become strong indeed. When they touch on their innermost guilty fears - the betrayal each suffered at the hands of the person he/she loved the most, we see the therapy of mutual confession, of shared grief and the comfort that comes from it. At long last, Billy's father's simple labelling becomes plain. Wavey is the Tall and Quiet Woman – the woman who waits patiently, who can be relied upon, who is modest and virtuous. She is in a sense the woman Quoyle always needed and wanted. And while the author does not strive to make a parallel, we cannot help thinking that Quoyle is to Wavey exactly the same thing – the Tall and Quiet Man.

Chapter 38   THE SLED DOG DRIVER'S DREAM

Yark is in his workshop finishing Quoyle's boat. Quoyle arrives saying that he and Wavey have spent the morning preparing food for the aunt's welcome home party. Yark sings his song and tells Quoyle that his boat will be ready the following Saturday. Yark works, and Quoyle, looking at the curved timbers, thinks of Wavey. He wonders if their ex-partners will continue to haunt them even if they marry.

At the party, Wavey plays her accordian and Dennis a guitar. There is a feeling of joviality and comaraderie. Bunny is desperate to show Quoyle something that Wavey has brought for them. Quoyle catches a smile from Wavey meant only for him as their eyes meet. Once again he wonders about love and its many shades and wonders whether it is possible to find another type of love, one that brings 'calm and pleasure' as opposed to love that induces the suffering with which he is familiar. Upstairs, Quoyle is surprised to see a husky puppy. Bunny can hardly form the words to say that it's a white dog. Bunny has ideas of getting a sled made, because she has decided she wants to be a 'dog-team racer' when she grows up. Bunny has named the dog 'Warren the Second'.

Downstairs Quoyle hugs the aunt and then Wavey. He kisses Wavey, and everybody takes this as an announcement. Wavey's father winks at Quoyle in approval. Billy Pretty arrives late and warns about the approaching storm.

During the night the storm rages. Bunny dreams that the old house on the Point is being ripped apart by the devastating wind. Quoyle responds to her screams, brings her warm milk, and explains the nightmare away as a product of the stormy weather.

Quoyle runs a special issue of *The Gammy Bird* documenting the effects of the storm. Wavey unexpectedly arrives at the newspaper office whispering to Quoyle that he must go by Archie's house at noon. As he approaches the house, Quoyle sees Wavey's father, binoculars in hand, scanning Quoyle's Point. The house is gone. Quoyle knows that the aunt will be deeply affected and he feels as though he has lost something too, lost a silent place. He feels that the Quoyles are on the move again. In Dennis' company snowmobile, Quoyle goes to the Point to see first-hand find the great bare rock.

Quoyle suggests buying the Burke's house. The aunt says she will never get over the loss of the house and Quoyle replies that she has managed to overcome worse. He tells the aunt that he knows what his father, her brother, did to her when they were children. Her life's secret revealed, the aunt weeps into her hands as Quoyle pats her on the shoulder. The aunt says they'll build a summer house out at the Point with the insurance money. She suggests he and Wavey and the children live in the Burke's house, as she is considering buying the shop and making an apartment upstairs. She and Mavis Bangs will live together.

The party for Aunt Agnis is another of Proulx's scenes of comical festivity. The warmth of friendship and family is hard to miss. Note in passing that Bunny has got over her fear of dogs, with the present of the husky puppy. Note that Quoyle is now able to kiss Wavey in public, a sign everyone takes as indicative of their intentions towards one another. It doesn't matter that a wild storm is raging outside, as often is the case in life, for inside, people are snug and warm in their personal relations. It doesn't matter really that the old Quoyle house has finally been blown off the cliff. Quoyle was never deeply attached to it. He does not need the house in any simple totemistic way to affirm his belonging. He now knows he belongs, deep down in his bones. The final knot perhaps is Quoyle telling the aunt that he knows her dreadful secret. His telling her is not in any way an accusation, but a reaching out of compassion and consulation. That the aunt weeps in front of Quoyle is part of her healing process.

Chapter 39   SHINING HUBCAPS

Yark has finished Quoyle's boat. Quoyle and Dennis heave it onto a trailer. Yark opens his mouth and Quoyle, anticipating Yark's song, breaks into the tune himself.

Quoyle and Wavey are dinner guests at Dennis and Beety's. Warren the Second lies under the table. Sunshine sings a rhyme. Bunny and Marty share a chair and choose a heart shaped lolly from a bag saved since Valentine's Day.

Dennis doesn't have any work, and Quoyle says he should work at the paper, but he scoffs at the idea. Beety mentions unenthusiastically that they are thinking about moving to Toronto for a couple of years to work and save some money. Quoyle can't tell his friends not to leave, but he knows that he will miss them tremendously and that they will probably never return.

While everyone else sleeps, Quoyle runs a bath. Towelling himself, he looks at his reflection in the mirror and takes in his immense form, with its overall image of 'strength [rather] than obesity'. He feels inexplicably joyous. In the middle of the night he is awoken by the phone. Jack has not returned since he set out to sea in the early hours of the morning. Dennis rings again at midnight. Jack caught his foot in a slingstone line and has drowned.

In the morning, Quoyle stops at the wharf on his way to pick up Wavey. Quoyle consoles her as she cries on his shoulder. Then they return to their respective tasks of making school lunches and driving the children to school. Quoyle senses a certain stillness and feels somewhat guilty that he is alive when Jack is dead.

Mrs Buggit and her sisters tend to Jack's corpse to prepare him for his funeral. Mrs Buggit is surprisingly calm; she has expected Jack to be drowned at sea ever since they were married. At least she has the comfort of burying the body, as was not the case with their son Jesson. Quoyle begins to organise a special edition of the paper 'dedicated to Jack'. To Benny Fudge's question about whether the paper will fold, he replies that 'a paper has a life of its own'.

Quoyle is exhausted and dreads seeing Jack dead. Bunny wants to go to the wake. Wavey thinks the children should go, but Quoyle feels that they should be protected 'from knowledge of death'. Nevertheless he agrees.

There is a large crowd in the Buggit house. Billy Pretty speaks poetically about the nature of life and death. Bunny has found a place near the coffin and sits staring at Jack's body. Dennis rummages around the kitchen searching for Jack's lodge pin which has been missing for years. As Mrs Buggit is pinning the brooch to Jack's lapel, in a wave of renewed tears and emotions on everyone's part, there is a cough, and Dennis shouts that Jack has come back. Quoyle watches as some help to pull Jack from the coffin. Bunny shouts that Jack's woken up. The guests celebrate the miracle of Jack's return. Dennis relates the doctor's explanation that immersion in icy water causes the heart rate to drop until it is barely perceptible. Dennis holds a pile of papers – forms for Jack to sign his lobster license over to Dennis.

In the spare room at the Buggit's, Wavey is talking to Bunny about death. She says that in some cases, mistakes are made, like in Jack's case. Wavey senses that Bunny's questioning is far from over, but Wavey knows that she will be there to try and explain in the future. Bunny wants to go to the rock where she had placed the dead bird. She and Wavey go there together and although there is no bird, Bunny finds a feather lying in the grass and thinks that the bird has flown away.

During the following weeks, Jack regains his strength. Quoyle and Wavey marry, and in the front yard of the Burke's house, Wavey's father erects a gleaming sculpture of hubcaps on sticks. Quoyle experiences the richness of life and comes to believe that if miracles like Jack's survival can occur, then he can be happy and experience love for a second time, without the suffering of his first time.

The final chapter offers us what appears to be a terrible tragedy. The apparent death of Jack is a shock to all, because he means so much to them. Even the joining together of his friends and family to acknowledge his life is strongly positive. That he is suddenly revealed to have been in hypothermic coma, and not dead at all, is a delightful joke played by the author on us, and subliminally a hint that life is not always as cruel as we might think.

The novel ends in a celebratory fashion. Bunny is now grappling positively with the notion of death, accepting that it is part of life. Quoyle and Wavey's marriage is the tangible sign of their love. In Quoyle's joyous sense of life not being always bitter, in his wonderment at being alive, and the possiblity of love, he sees an affirmative view of life – a view that the author also commends to us.

CHARACTERS, THEMES AND ISSUES

CHARACTERS

Quoyle

The central character, Quoyle, is a wonderfully dynamic portrait, of a man who changes significantly in the course of the narrative. Much of the point of *The Shipping News* is what happens to Quoyle. He is not the only interesting character, but we need to be very much aware of where he has come from and where he ends up if we are to understand the central 'message' of Proulx's work.

Quoyle begins, so far as we get to know him in the text, virtually as a hopeless case. He is naive, passive, ugly, clumsy, a chronic under-achiever. His father's contempt and brother's scorn have left him with little or no belief in himself. His capacity for love is not reciprocated. His marriage to the merciless Petal convinces him of his unworthiness, though we as readers cannot help noticing that it is Petal who has little to commend her. Her running away tells Quoyle that he is a hopeless husband as well as a father. His lack of friends (except for Partridge), his dismissal from the newspaper job, and then the sudden shocking death of Petal, all combine to give him the impression that life is cruel, that his fate is to suffer, and that survival is all one can expect.

The move to Newfoundland exposes him however to other influences. Primary amongst these is Agnis Hamm, 'the aunt'. Her benign influence, together with his gradual exposure to decent, simple folk in the community he joins, his slow-dawning infatuation with Wavey, his 'adoption' into the Buggit family, all begin to rehabilitate him. Gradually, Quoyle comes to have a new found sense of worth. His job at *The Gammy Bird*, though it has an inauspicious beginning, convinces him that he can write.

He begins to see that he is a successful father, and that Bunny's problems are neither insurmountable nor unusual – not his fault, but the natural consequences of her age and the traumas she has been through. Most importantly perhaps, he begins to find in his relationship with Wavey a sense of renewed confidence that he can be a man in relation to a woman. Their developing love affair is a central part of his rehabilitation.

It is more complex still than this. Quoyle is forced to confront the sordid nature of his family past – containing as it does shipwreckers, pirates, incestuous brothers and misfits of various kinds. Yet even this confrontation is a beneficial one. When he finds himself able to be reconciled, however awkwardly, to his half-crazy cousin Nolan, he comes to a point of acknowledgement of his heritage. By the end of the novel, Quoyle is capable of self-assertion, self-confidence and a form of happiness. That he remains such an oddball character, so little like a traditional hero, that he is such an ordinary guy, helps the author articulate the idea that reconciliation and rehabilitation are possible for every individual. Quoyle, at once a beautifully complex and well realised character, and an emblem of the human spirit in search of happiness, is central to our understanding of this fine novel.

Agnis Hamm

Unlike Quoyle, who changes significantly between the time we first meet him and the end of the novel, 'the aunt' remains essentially throughout the text the same character. She is solid, competent, confident. Certainly her stony isolation is mellowed by her involvement with Quoyle and his two children. When she admits, after an absence, 'I've missed every one of you. Badly.', it marks a realisation in her that her family (Quoyle and the girls) has become a key part of her life. Her sharing in Quoyle's existence, with its ups and downs, its freaky surprises and irritations, brings her back into contact with a life which, after her childhood traumas and the loss of Irene Warren, she had begun to doubt somewhat. She finds herself needed, however, by a real family, and blossoms because of it.

At heart, Agnis represents the capacity of human nature to survive. Despite having been sexually abused, and rejected by her family as a young woman, despite loneliness and the traumatic loss of her lover, Agnis comes through. As she says in Chapter 28, she has learnt how to 'manage'! This is crucial. Her confidence, her ability to succeed, her resilient spirit which survives no matter what, like the old house on the windswept point of which she is so fond, is in itself a model for Quoyle, who learns how to be a more resilient and happier human being.

Wavey Prowse

Wavey is not only the novel's 'love interest'. She is also emblematic. She becomes Quoyle's model of warm-heartedness. This first becomes apparent in her devotion to her handicapped son, and in the support group she has helped form for others in her position. It then becomes clear that she is capable of 'adopting' Quoyle's children, caring for them and loving them the way she does her own son. Unlike Petal, Quoyle's first wife, who was pretty, sexy and vivacious, but inwardly shallow, if not disturbed –

Wavey has all the traditional virtues of womanhood. She is modest, graceful, thoughtful, nurturing and loving. She doesn't judge Quoyle on his external appearance, which is far from glamorous, but sees instead the beautiful inner qualities he possesses. She lets go of her love for Herold (just as Quoyle lets go of his love for Petal), accepting Quoyle as her lover and soulmate. Quoyle's happiness in finding her we understand to be reciprocated in her happiness in finding a man who truly loves her. Just as Quoyle embodies the author's positive vision of a possibility for human happiness, so the same thing is reflected, modestly but importantly, in her portrait of Wavey too.

Jack Buggit

We primarily see Jack as Quoyle's mentor. Although the Quoyle family history is against him, Jack doesn't reject Quoyle when he applies for the job on *The Gammy Bird*. He accepts him, gives him a chance, and it pays off. We are led to believe that Jack is a very intuitive individual. When, against all expectation, Quoyle begins to show a flair for writing, Jack acknowledges his potential and rewards him. This transformation culminates in Jack making him editor of *The Gammy Bird*. Jack is someone else who sees beyond superficial appearances, to the real human potential in an individual.

There is more to Jack however, albeit hinted at rather than described in literal detail. Jack has something of the qualities of a wise man or seer. He seems to be to some extent in touch with the supernatural, having what might loosely be called 'second sight', being able to 'see' when people are in trouble at sea. Even at *The Gammy Bird*, he seems to intuitively tap the community's subconscious, not to mention the subconscious of his writers. He understands what the writers and the community fear, and forces them, not out of malice but out of some deep instinct for betterment, to face those fears and move on.

What are we to make of Jack's hilarious 'resurrection' at the end of the story? At one level, it is the author playing a delightful joke on the reader. At another level, it perhaps evokes symbolically the idea that life is more benign sometimes than we expect, that people often do get a second chance. At the very least, it suggests that fate is inexplicable – a man thought dead may miraculously survive against all the odds. It may be criticised by some readers as too implausible, but will no doubt be accepted by most as a clever twist which helps contribute in its modest way towards the 'upbeat' feel of the book's ending.

Petal Bear

Quoyle's first wife is manipulative, a hedonist, cold, and untrustworthy. Her preoccupations are sex, money and fun. While we are never granted insight into her background and why she might be as she is, and may possibly be judging her unfairly, she does not come across well. The very least we can say about Petal is that she appears to be quite amoral. What sort of a mother sells her small children to a paedophile?

She contrasts Quoyle's ultimate affirmation of self, self-confidence and happiness with a representation of that which is destructive, malign and unhappy. She embodies the forces of human nature from which Quoyle is in part descended and which he (and others) strive to rise above. She is a femme fatale of almost comic ferocity. Although her memory haunts the unfortunate Quoyle, she acts within the scheme of the novel more as a representative of the brutal aspects of human nature than anything else.

THEMES AND ISSUES

The storm of life - fear, fate, and tragedy in human existence

Although it is possible to think of *The Shipping News* as comic, it is black comedy. Proulx takes an often perverse interest in the bleak possibilies of fate.

Consider the symbolism of *The Gammy Bird*. Its staple diet comprises sexual abuse stories, car accidents, shipwreck and gossip (the dirtier the better). Many of the ads are fake. It routinely gulls the public with file car wrecks presented as news. The whole enterprise was a scheme to get its proprietor off the dole.

Quite a number of the episodes in the plot make heavy reading. Quoyle's mother and father commit suicide, his brother rejects him, his wife is killed in a horrific accident, having sold her children to a pervert. Quoyle nearly drowns. Agnis Hamm was sexually abused as a child, more than once; her lover died of cancer; her dog dies. Old Nolan Quoyle lives an impoverished existence in a ghost town with only a dog for company, going slowly mad. Jack Buggit lost his elder son to the sea, and nearly drowns, himself. Nutbeem was sexually abused as a child; his beloved boat is destroyed by drunks. Billy Pretty's long-suffering father died young. Melville is murdered by his wife and her lover, his head severed and his body cut into pieces. Wavey's husband mistreated her; he died at sea; her only child is intellectually handicapped. The book abounds with instances of life's tragic potential. Even when nothing happens, the possibility that it might, haunts the characters. After hearing about Billy Pretty's father, Quoyle reacts thus:

> Quoyle's eyes moist, imagining his little daughters, orphaned, travelling across the cold continent to a savage farmer.

So used is he to life's storms, of which he has encountered so many, that he expects tragedy.

Proulx may offer us some grim humour, but she also leaves us in little doubt that life is not all sweetness and light. Just as she brilliantly portrays the stormy, frigid coastline of Newfoundland, so she gives us heart-stopping glimpses of how vicious destiny can be. No one in this text is immune to heartbreak. Even the children have nightmares. Bunny keeps seeing the 'white dog' (of death?), which, though it turns out to be a real dog, still operates as a kind of symbol of nameless dread. Even on a summer's day, mending the roof, death is only seconds away, and the sea's apparent moods of calm are succeeded by fog, storm, ice. Proulx is too subtle to stop there. Her vision of existence is complex, contradictory, because life is like that. But we should not be lulled by the 'fairy tale' quality of the story into seeing all life as benign. The very warmth of the novel's redemptions is set against the chill dark of its miseries.

Identity and self-esteem

'I know something now that I didn't a year ago,' said Quoyle. 'Petal wasn't any good. And I think maybe that is why I loved her.'

'Yes,' said Wavey. 'Same with Herold. It's like you feel to yourself that's all you deserve. And the worse it gets the more it seems true, that you got it coming to you or it wouldn't be that way. You know what I mean?'

We know what she means, for it is a universal theme. A person can carry from their childhood or early experiences with other adults such a terrible sense of not being worthy that it cripples them throughout life. It is one of the novel's key themes.

In Quoyle's case, unsympathetic parents, a callous brother, and the handicap of a 'different' appearance have conspired to make him feel inadequate – as a person, a worker, a man. Everything he touches seems to fall apart. He is accident-prone and unlucky. Wavey too has a problem with feeling good about herself, largely at the hands of her cruel husband. When Quoyle gets to Newfoundland, he discovers that his family past is anything but pleasant. He finds out about the ancestors 'whose filthy blood ran in his veins, who murdered the shipwrecked, drowned their unwanted brats, fought and howled...' His father committed incest. His oldest living relative is crazy.

The good news is that low self-esteem need not be a life-long sentence. Identity can be reshaped, given positive experiences and the therapy of good relationships. In finding that he can be a competent writer, that he can attract the loving attentions of a good woman, that he is not a failure as a parent, but a considerable success, that he can cope with the pressures and demands of family – Quoyle reconstitutes his sense of self. The qualified optimism of the ending is a tribute to hope, but also to the transforming power of positive self-image. Without once mentioning psychotherapeutic jargon (such as 'positive self-image'), Proulx nonetheless sets us up to understand the importance in a person's life of how he feels about himself. A good self-image, and life can be joyous. A bad one, and it can be like an endless winter storm.

The possibility of redemption and survival

The narrative structure of *The Shipping News* is a simple one. A loser goes back to his roots, and finds love. He is reborn as a happy man.

Put so bluntly, it sounds appallingly crude. Yet one of the virtues of the novel is to make the slow transformation of Quoyle utterly believable and to render it in such poetic language, with such a subtle sense of spirituality combined with earthy charm, that we accept it as true. A man who felt life had dealt him nothing but bad cards, whose lot seemed to be misery, comes to joy. It is the joy of a simple man, but that doesn't stop it from being a complex and wonderful thing. Consider the scene in which Quoyle lies on the clifftop looking after Wavey. He sees in that moment of insight not only that his life is entwined with Wavey's, but that he and she and all the people he loves are part of a larger whole. He sees the Quoyles 'rinsed of evil' and understands that 'events [are] in trembling balance'. A state of grace descends upon him and he knows that life is good, no matter how many storms may come and go.

Whence comes this possibility of grace? Proulx never mentions religion. Nor has she any interest in trendy therapies (the only mention of mental counselling is the satiric one in Nolan's glee at conning the people at the mental home). She certainly believes in the power of fellowship and love to heal. But there is more.

First there is the cycle of nature. When Quoyle looks after Wavey he sees not just her figure in the distance, and that of his aunt and daughters, but also the earth, the rocks, the sea – the elements, time (he sees the past washed clean, and his own happy future), perhaps the cosmos itself – the life force. There is a subliminal hint in Proulx's descriptions of seasons that people's lives are the same. Like summer succeeding winter, like children coming after their parents, life goes on. Bad experiences (like the storms and drownings) are not all that it offers us. There are storms, but there are also parties, and weddings, and moments of joy. Once the characters learn to trust in the process of life, fate brings them happier circumstances. Once they cease dwelling on their fears, Proulx seems to suggest, positives can be found.

Second there is the amazing tenacity of people. Just as the Newfoundlanders have to confront the sea, and survive it, so people have to face life's traumas and find the will to go on. 'We face up to awful things because we can't go around them,' advises Aunt Agnis. 'The sooner...you say, "Yes, it happened, and there's nothing I can do about it," the sooner you can get on with your own life.' Like Quoyle thrown into the icy sea, but hanging on until rescued, people can survive. Enduring, 'managing', homely wisdom though it may be, is part of what Proulx is offering. It is a view of life which embraces stark contrasts, but overall finds a great deal to celebrate.

Family and heredity - the complex knots of kin

Quoyle comes from what we can only describe as a dysfunctional family. He moves on to a seriously bad marriage. His children at times seem twisted, if not a bit feral. His aunt was sexually abused by her brother, Quoyle's father. The old Quoyles were pirates and shipwreckers, mad and bad. He keeps on getting worse shocks as he traces his roots. Old Nolan hates Quoyle enough to put a curse on him. Meanwhile, Jack and Dennis seem to have fallen out. Herold Prowse cheated on Wavey. Silver Melville kills her husband. The pages of *The Gammy Bird* regularly relate the tales of incest and abuse that appear to be part of Newfoundland life. We can't say that Proulx's view of family is a starry-eyed one.

Yet the book also acknowledges the pull of family. Like so many other central aspects of human life, family is not one thing or another. It can scar but it can also heal. It is one of the 'knots' which binds people to one another, and to life. A large part of Nolan's problem is his solitude - which is at least partly remedied by the coming of his younger kin. The stoical old aunt is mellowed by her contact with Quoyle and his offspring. Her admission that she missed them is a small detail but a big moment. At its best, as in the warm Buggit household (several times rhapsodically described), or in the scenes involving Quoyle playing with his daughters, or in Wavey's unconditional love of Herry, we see the enormous power for good of kinship. The extended family which Quoyle joins in courting and then marrying Wavey (Herry, Ken, Oscar, Archie, old Yark and his wife) becomes part of him too. The wake for Jack which finishes the novel is a comic turn (given his resurrection), but it also reminds us of this key element in Proulx's depiction of life – that family is central, for better or (sometimes) worse.

The virtues of simple people

One of the minor characters who seems at first like a 'walk-on extra', another of Proulx quaint Newfoundlanders, but who appears again and again, is Alvin Yark. What is Yark? A boatbuilder, an old world craftsman, who out of his deep knowledge of the sea, constructs boats that are not only safe, but also works of art. He sings as he works and shows young Quoyle his craft.

The boatbuilder, the fisherman (Jack), the carpenter (Dennis), the upholsterer (Agnis), the harbourmaster (Diddy) – these are important characters in *The Shipping News*. Not one is well educated. Not a soul is famous, outside their tiny isolated communities. Yet in them reside a good part of the author's hint that small town folk know a great deal. Quoyle, the only one who has been to college, doesn't teach them – he learns from them. When he attends their hammy, unsophisticated Christmas Pageant, he comes away knowing something the bonds of community. When he finally understands why Jack has set his reporters their bizarre beats, he sees the deeper wisdom in apparently crazy behaviour.

These simple people are not caricatures the author has set up for us to laugh at (though they are amusing at times) – but individuals in touch with life. They understand that skill, hard work, loyalty, love and endurance are important. Life is short and its good moments are to be enjoyed. Too much thinking is not useful. Talk is for companionship. Marriage and family are central to happiness. In such simple, old fashioned ideas the author finds wisdom, and offers it to us too.

The knot of love

The novel ends, as has been observed, with a reference to love. This is no accident. Love has been one of Proulx's major themes.

She plays a number of variations on it. We have love between a man and woman, family love, even the affection of people for dogs (in Agnis' attachment to Warren, and finally, Bunny's new puppy). We have friendship, which is a lighter shade of the same thing. We have love that hurts (Quoyle and Petal, Wavey and Herold), love that irritates (Agnis and Bunny), and of course love that transforms (Quoyle and Wavey).

Quoyle's very name is a play on the idea of a knot – 'coil'. His whole story is a play on the theme of love. Whom does he love? The Maids in the Meadow (Bunny and Sunshine), the Demon Lover (Petal), the Stouthearted Woman (Agnis) and the Tall and Quiet Woman (Wavey). Like different knots, his love for them is different, and it affects him differently. Love makes him what he is. It binds him, strengthens him, ties him to life. The Quoyle at the beginning is floating loose, his life unravelling. The Quoyle at the end is connected, by love knots, and a happy man. Although it is a simple metaphor, the knot motif is a key one, and central to the novel's message of hope.

WHAT DO THE CRITICS SAY?

Newfoundland is the real subject of Proulx's stunning novel, in which the reader is assaulted by a rich, down-in-the-dirt, up-in-the-skies prose full of portents, repetitions, bold metaphors, brusque dialogues and set pieces of great beauty. The characters are radiant with life, but, flung against the drumrolls of rain, the cracking floes and dard skies of an elemental landscape, they are also emblematic.

(*Contemporary Literary Criticism*, Vol.81)

Proulx's deliberately choppy prose is the perfect vehicle for a style chockablock with epigrammatic statements, metaphors and world-defining catalogs....Both the economy and the imaginative excess of [character's like Tert Card] suggest the paradoxical virtues of Proulx's style. A style with such energy of its own can detract from the story, but not here. Each of the multitude of characters introduced in the first half of the book plays a role in the accelerating plot. What at first seems to be episodic, twists into a complicated knot of story. The payoff in the novel's scheme of knots could not be more satisfying. It takes a little patience at the beginning, but *The Shipping News* turns into a wonderful novel.

(Suzanne Keen, Review in *Commonweal*, 2 December 1994)

In less capable hands, Quoyle's eventual reconciliation with the ocean and his past could have become a long string of saccharine bummers. But although Quoyle is decidedly melancholy, the book's tone is anything but dolorous.

The comic edge Proulx forces on Quoyle's saga can sometimes grate. The fanciful names she gives her characters – Sparkly Fudge, Al Catalog, Diddy Shovel, Wavey Prowse – turn too many important moments into cartoon panels.

Quoyle's plight, however, doesn't feel trivialised or exaggerated. Rarely in contemporary fiction has a writer so knowingly explored what Nietzsche described, in his chilling aphorism, as the brute recognition that "terrible experiences give one cause to speculate whether the one who experiences them may not be something terrible." In Proulx's earlier work, such haunting speculation drives her characters to violent ends, leaving us abuzz with helpless sympathy and horror. If *The Shipping News* is a more affirming and less astringent saga, its picture of a man wracked by his demons lives frighteningly in the mind. That Quoyle survives his contaminants seems a small and real gift. When the grotesque sins of the father are visited upon his son, he gives, heartily, as good as he gets.

(Dwight Garner, 'Northeastern Exposure', in *VLS*, No 114, April, 1993)

An early traveler's account of the Maritime Provinces says, 'After but a year's visit, one is convinced that the sea has a savage appetite for Newfoundlanders.' In E. Annie Proulx's vigorous, quirky novel *The Shipping News*, set in present-day Newfoundland, there are indeed a lot of drownings. The main characters are plagued by dangerous undercurrents, both in the physical world and in their own minds. But the local color, ribaldry and uncanny sorts of redemption of Ms Proulx's third book of fiction keep the reader from slipping under, into the murk of loss. The novel, largely set in the village of Killick-Claw, along Newfoundland's foggy, storm-battered coast, displays Ms Proulx's surreal humor and her zest for the strange foibles of humanity.

Happily for the reader, Ms Proulx keeps returning to the offices of *The Gammy Bird*. As Quoyle's gypsy family moves from house to trailer, the office becomes his home base. There he meets the staff, true brigands of outback journalism. It is also where the pitch of Ms Proulx's writing is most finely turned. Their spontaneous monologues, when spiced with the local patois, are wonderfully performed riffs of nostalgia, anecdote, indictment and complaint that strike us as Newfoundland's most rollicking oral literature.

Throughout *The Shipping News*, the sinuousness of E. Annie Proulx's prose seems to correspond physically with the textures of the weather and sea. Her inventive language is finely, if exhaustively, accomplished. If I have any complaint it is that at times she carries her own brond of poetic compression too far: 'Billy's worn shape down to the bones, cast Quoyle as a sliding mass.' Weather off shore or overland can often seem chokingly imbued with portentousness. Near the novel's end, Jack Buggit sits-up in his own coffin, spouting water, having both drowned and not drowned; it is a forced invention in a novel otherwise replete with wonderfully natural ones.

Ms Proulx is never too showy with her research, though *The Shipping News* is almost an encyclopedia of slang and lore. The way her Newfoundlanders talk, the most factual account seems as high-spirited as gossip over a supper of snow crab, cod cheeks, lobster salad and seal-flipper stew.

(Howard Norman, Review in *The New York Times Book Review*, April 4, 1993)

Proulx is not above throwing in the odd extreme [in her fiction]. [This work] includes storms at sea, premonitory dreams, decapitations, rescues and resuscitation of a drowned man during his own wake. Perhaps even more improbably, the battered Quoyle acquire genuine dignity and worth by hard work at a job that he learns to love-turning the shipping news of a small local paper into a column taken seriously by other journalists.

Proulx's triumph is that she makes us swallow all of this. Her work not only describes, but is imbued with, a chancy decency that looks us forthright in the eye and challenges disbelief. This is an artful novel. Proulx takes us to a land of myth–Quoyle is at one level the Holy Fool who does not know how to ask the right questions– and urban legend, full of the things we want or fear to believe in.

What risks being mere whimsy has steel behing it, because there is passion here and a real potential for tragedy. There is precise intelligence, a sense of how small communities work and of how power is divided within them.

(Rox Kaveney, 'Local Hero', in *New Statesman & Society*, December 3, 1993)

WHAT SHOULD A RESPONSE LOOK LIKE?...
A SAMPLE ESSAY

'And it may be that love sometimes occurs without pain or misery.'

The Shipping News suggests that love, however desirable, is never easy.

Discuss.

Quoyle worries about love. Even when it seems to be dawning again, with Wavey, he can't believe it. "Not love, which wrenched and wounded. Not love, which came only once." To him, love is an emotional bobby trap – months of "fiery happiness" followed by years of suffering. What he feels for Wavey can't be love because it feels so safe and comfortable. What he felt for Petal was love, because it crucified him. In what is almost a black joke about the miseries of romance, E. Annie Proulx offers us a hero who has been scarred by love, and must slowly regain his confidence in the most famous ideal of all.

Quoyle's misadventures with love undoubtedly go back to his childhood, like his other problems. Just as his chronic lack of self-esteem relates to his being held in contempt by his father and brother, so his acceptance of Petal's mistreatment relates to him not feeling good enough to be loved. Later, Wavey will put it beautifully after their mutual confession of their betrayed love affairs with their dead spouses. "It's like you feel to yourself," she says, speaking of the promiscuous and cruel Herold, "that's all you deserve." No joining of equals, but a mismatched, desperate, foolish thing. Quoyle understands that his earlier 'stupid self' took whatever it could get, so far as love was concerned. "No wonder love shot him through the heart and lungs, caused internal bleeding." So, when Petal half-jokingly seduces him and accepts his sincere offer of marriage as a trophy, he falls into a dreadful trap.

His short but agonised relationship with Petal seems to confirm his, and our, worst fears about love. The lover suffers, burns, is broken-hearted. In the words of the old song, the pleasure of love lasts only a moment; the pain of love lasts for ever. His months of ecstasy become years of agony. Petal seems the very ideal – the pretty, sexy, vivacious Demon Lover, and he accepts all her cruelties in the name of love. Her death devastates him, no matter how cruelly she had mistreated him. In life, she tortured him. In death, her ghost torments him still. In his daughter Bunny he sees the image of Petal, and his heart breaks again.

Yet Petal is not the only type of woman there is, and his fiery marriage to her is not the only form of love. The return to Newfoundland brings him back to simpler people. One of them is the humble widowed fisherman's wife, and single mother, Wavey. In contrast to Petal's whirlwind seduction, Quoyle and Wavey's courtship takes months, proceeding from glances, to shared moments, to an awkward grappling on the clifftop meadow, and only finally to bed and marriage. In Wavey, Quoyle finds a "Tall and Quiet Woman", modest, compassionate, silently loving. He can't quite believe in what they find, it seems so gentle and sweet. Can happiness coexist with love? Can passion happen a second time, and to one who thinks himself so unworthy?

Proulx is not slipping into comicbook romance. Even while celebrating it, she hints that love is not easy. Quoyle may be together with Wavey, but the ghosts of the past remain to haunt them. Both of them are damaged by the past, and shy about their newfound relationship. On the clifftop, Wavey makes a defensive speech about poor drowned Herold. When they finally embrace in the hotel bed, she reveals that this was where she had her honeymoon, and the betrayal began. Quoyle has flashbacks to his passionate if wretched life with Petal. Wavey still has her handicapped son to worry about. Quoyle still has his daughters. Love hasn't solved all of life's problems. But it has made existence easier.

For the most part, The Shipping News takes an affirmative view of love. The central romance is the focus of our interest, but all around are gentle reminders of the theme. "I've missed every one of you. Badly," says Aunt Agnis to the children, after a separation. Dennis and Beety's home is a happy one. Even the Buggit wake, though a comic set piece, is testimony to family love. The pain is real at Jack's imagined death, and the pleasure even more so at the discovery that he is alive once more. Love of Petal put Quoyle through agonies. Love of Bunny made him tremble when she nearly fell off the ladder, and when he worries for her disturbances. But his continued capacity for love also rehabilitates him. It brings him to Wavey, and happiness. Overall, love binds and strengthens more than it breaks. It is desirable because it offers, for all its pains and occasional betrayals, one of the principal comforts of life.